Tears *of* Blood

Tears *of* Blood

Selected Verses of GHALIB

Translated from Urdu by

Sunil Uniyal

PARTRIDGE
A Penguin Random House Company

Copyright © 2014 by Sunil Uniyal.

ISBN:	Softcover	978-1-4828-3435-2
	eBook	978-1-4828-3444-4

To order additional copies of this book, contact
Partridge India
000 800 10062 62
orders.india@partridgepublishing.com

www.partridgepublishing.com/india

In memory of my Father

Contents

Preface 13

Part I

1 *Phir mujhe deed-e-tar yaad aayaa* 18
  Those moist eyes have come to my mind once again
2 *Arz-e-niyaaz-e-ishq ke kaabil nahin rahaa* 20
  Love entreaties I can't make any more
3 *Mahram naheen hai tu hee navaahaa-e-raaz kaa* 22
  The voice of His mystery is to you an alien thing
4 *Zikr us pareevash kaa, aur phir bayaan apnaa* 24
  The mention in my own style of that angelic beauty
5 *Yeh na thee hamaari kismet ki visaal-e-yaar hotaa* 26
  A union with the Beloved was not in my fate
6 *Na thaa kuchch, to Khudaa thaa,* 28
  God was when there wasn't anything
7 *Darkhure kahro gazab jab koyi hamsaa na huaa* 30
  Slander and torture in love when
  none has borne like me
8 *Balaa se hain ye jo pesh-e-nazar dar-o-deevaar* 32
  Trouble bearing before my eyes
  are these doors and walls
9 *Laraztaa hai miraa dil zehmat-e-* 34
  mehar-e-darakhshaan par
  My heart shudders at the rise of Sun at dawn
10 *Kyon jal gayaa na taab-e-rukh-e-yaar dekhkar* 36
  Why has the glow of Beloved's face not burnt me?

11 *Ghar jab banaa liyaa tere dar par kahe bighair* 38
When without your consent, at
your door I'm residing,

12 *Laazim thaa ki dekho miraa rastaa koyi din aur* 40
You didn't consider it necessary to wait a few days more

13 *Na gul-e-nagmah hoon, na pardah-e-saaz* 42
I am no musical tone, no song blossoming

14 *Rukhe nigaar se hai soz-e-jaavidaani-e-shamma* 44
The face of the Beloved is a candle eternally glowing

15 *Zakhm par chhirrken kahaan
tiphlaane—beparvaa namak* 46
Where are all the carefree kids who
on my wounds can spill salt?

16 *Jahaan teraa naqsh-e-kadam dekhte hain* 48
Wherever your footprints I see

17 *Maane-e-dashtnavardee koyi tadbeer naheen* 50
Nothing can stop me from desert-wandering

18 *Vo firaaq aur vo visaal kahaan?* 52
Where are those meetings and those partings now?

19 *Maze jahaan ke apnee nazar men khaaq naheen* 54
In my eyes, the pleasures of the
world are nothing at all

20 *Kee vafaa hamse to ghair usko jafaa kahte hain* 56
When she shows her love to me,
others say she is unfaithful

21 *Hairaan hoon dil ko rovoon ki peetoon jigar ko mai* 58
Should I cry my heart out or beat
my chest - I am confused

22 *Daayim parraa huaa tire dar par naheen hoon main* 60
I wish I were forever lying at Your doorstep,

23 *Dono jahaan de ke vo samjhaa yeh khush rahaa* 62
He gifted me both the worlds and
thought I would be happy

24 *Sab kahaan, kuchh laal-o-gul
men numaayaa ho gayeen* 64
Few, very few are as roses or tulips returning

25 *Dil hee to hai, na sang-o-khisht,
dard se bhar na aaye kyoon?* 66
It's my heart, no brick or stone, why
won't it be filled with grief?

26 *Rahiye ab aisee jagah chalkar, jahaan koyee na ho* 68
Let us go to live where nobody else is there

27 *Kisi ko deke dil koyee navaa sanje phugaan kyoon ho?* 70
When my heart I have surrendered,
why should I utter cries of pain?

28 *Junoon tohmat kash-e-taskeen na
ho, gar shaadmaanee kee* 72
Why blame my frenzy in love, if it
seeks comfort in rejoicing

29 *Aa ki mere jaan ko qaraar naheen hai* 74
Come, Beloved, no peace I'm having

30 *Har qadam doori-e-manzil hai numaayaan mujhse* 76
At every step, my goal goes farther

31 *Ek jaa harf-e-vafaa likkhaa thaa so bhee mit gayaa* 78
The word 'love' in your letter has proved to be false

32 *Shabnam ba gul-e-laalah na khaali zi adaa hai* 80
The tear-drop on a poppy has, indeed, some meaning

33 *Miri hastee fazaa-e-hairat aabaad-e-tamannaa hai* 82
An open expanse of amazement, full
of longing, is my existence

34 *Muddat huvee hai yaar ko mehmaan kiye huve*   84
An age has passed since I hosted my Beloved

35 *Koyi ummeed bar naheen aatee*   86
My hopes bear no fruit anymore

36 *Dil-e-naadaan tujhe huaa kyaa hai?*   88
O naive heart, what the matter is?

37 *Har ek baat pe kahte ho tum ki tu kyaa hai?*   90
Whenever I say something, you say 'Who are you?'

38 *Ibn-e-Mariyam huaa kare koyi*   92
Like Mary's Son, may someone be

39 *Us bazm men mujhe naheen bantaa hayaa kiye*   94
In your assembly my self-esteem has no clout

40 *Baazeechaa-e-atfaal hai duniyaa, mire aage*   96
This world is a kids' playground to me,

41 *Bahot sahee gham-e- getee, sharaab kam kyaa hai*   100
The world is full of sorrow, but
where's the dearth of wine?

42 *Kunj men baithaa rahoon, yoon par khulaa*   102
I wish I was resting free in a garden

Part II

43 *Havas ko hai nishaat-e-kaar kyaa kyaa*   106
From desire many joys of action spring,

44 *Ghar hamaaraa jo na rote bhee to veeraan hotaa*   108
My house would have been a wilderness
even if I had not shed tears

45 *Huee taakheer to kuchh baais-e-taakheer bhee thaa*   110
You are late - for this delay, there
must be a reason sure

46 *Dard minnat-e-kash davaa na huaa* 112
My suffering has no panacea

47 *Aah ko chaahiye ik umra asar hone tak* 114
My sigh will need a lifetime indeed to have its effect

48 *Gham naheen hotaa hai aazaadon ko vesh az yak nafas* 116
Grief with we liberated ones, doesn't
stay for more than a breath

49 *Meherbaan hoke bulaa lo mujhe chaaho jis vaqt* 118
Be kind to call me anytime that you please

50 *Kal ke liye kar aaj na khissat sharaab men* 120
For your tomorrow, don't skip your drink today,

51 *Gham-e-duniyaa se, gar payee thee
fursat, sar uthaane kee* 122
If I had time to lift my head from the woes of the world

52 *Kyaa tang ham sitam zadgaan kaa jahaan hai* 124
The world of we distressed ones, is too narrow

53 *Masjid ke zer-e-saayah kharaabaat chaahiye* 126
As near a mosque, a wine-house is necessary

54 *Ishq mujhko nahin, vahshat hi sahee* 128
Yes, my love is not love, it's madness,

55 *Be-etidaaliyon se, subuk sab men ham hue* 130
My excesses in love have debased me

56 *Fariyaad kee koyi lai naheen hai* 132
A prayer may not necessarily have a melody,

57 *Rone se aur ishq men bebaak ho gaye* 134
We wept and opened up further in love

58 *Kab vo suntaa hai kahaanee meree* 136
When does He listen to my tale ?

59 *Dil se teri nigaah jigar tak utar gayee* 138
Your glance has pierced my heart and liver

60 *Naved-e-amna hai bedaad-e-dost jaan ke liye*   140
    Beloved's tyranny is a road I gladly walk
61 *Main unhen chherroon aur kuchh na kahen*   142
    I tease her, she says nothing – what a surprise!
62 *Hazaaron khvaahishen aisi, ki har*   144
    khvaahish pe dam nikle
    A thousand desires I had, each
    enough to take my breath

Part III

Selected Shers   148-178

Preface

Mirza Muhammad Asadullah Khan 'Ghalib', whose earlier pen-name was 'Asad', composed verse both in Urdu and Persian. He is acknowledged by many as the greatest master of Urdu ghazal and holds the same position in Urdu poetry as Kalidas in Sanskrit and Milton in English. He belonged to the line of aTurkish military commander, who had migrated to Agra from Samarkand in Central Asia to seek employment under the Later Mughals. It was at Agra that Ghalib was born in 1797 and had his education, but after his marriage in a noble family of Delhi at the age of 13 years, he shifted to Delhi around 1812 and lived there till his death on 15th February, 1869.

Ghalib belonged to an age when the Mughal Empire had been reduced to a pale shadow of its glorious past and the British power was growing unchecked all over India. The old order was ringing out, a new order was ringing in, and the situation presented a dilemma, which is so well reflected in Ghalib's poetry. Ghalib was a witness to the Great Revolt of 1857 and the tragic events that overwhelmed Delhi in its aftermath. A lot of innocent blood was shed during the upheaval and much of the Mughal Delhi was razed to the ground including the mansions and shops of Ghalib's close friends and acquaintances. Moreover, he had to suffer confinement within his own house for the period of the turmoil. The British atrocities during and after the Great Revolt, shook Ghalib to the core. In his prose work, *Dastanbuy*, he writes that 'beyond the (Chandni) Chowk, mass slaughter was rampant and the streets were filled with horror.' Many of his friends and relatives in the nobility were executed or exiled. The last of the Mughals, Bahadur Shah Zafar, who was himself an eminent poet and a patron of poets including Ghalib, was convicted by the British for his complicity in the revolt and deported to Rangoon (Burma) where he died a forlorn prisoner in the year 1862.

Ghalib's own life was marked by a string of tragedies. He lost his father when he was only 4 years of age and came under the guardianship of his uncle, but he too died in a couple of years, leaving Ghalib at the mercy of his in-laws. He had seven children from marriage but sadly none of them survived, and even an adopted son met the same fate.He had a mentally challenged brother who was killed, perhaps mistakenly, in a commotion in the city of Delhi in the year 1857. Ghalib was also not without vices. He was excessively fond of gambling and drinking with friends and frequented the salons of courtesans, but having no regular income, except a monthly pension of Rs. 62.50, he was constantly short of money and increasingly became insolvent on account of his reckless way of living. He fought a protracted battle with the British authorities for increase in his pension, but his efforts ultimately came to nought. All these events left him with a permanent feeling of hurt and dismay.

Ghalib's poetry seems to be in sync with his tragic times. His ghazals mirror the vulnerability of Man, his unfulfilled longings, his broken promises, his loneliness and sense of loss and grief, as well as his soul's yearning for Eternal Beauty and Love. Ghalib is, thus, a poet for all times.Though his own age was not very appreciative of his poetry, he was confident that one day he would be able to get his due. In his own words: "My star was shining highest in the sky before my birth; my poetry is going to win the world's acclaim after I am dead." Time is, indeed, proving him right.

In these poetic translations (at times, transcreations) of selected Urdu verse of Ghalib, I have consulted the *Divaan-e-Ghalib* published by the Ghalib Institute, New Delhi, in Devanagri Hindi, as I am not conversant with the Urdu script. For difficult Urdu words, the Urdu-Hindi Dictionary edited by Acharya Ramchandra Verma and published by Shabdlok Prakashan, Varanasi, has been my frequent guide. I am also indebted to the works of other translators of Ghalib, especially Aijaz Ahmad, Sarfaraz Niazi, Kuldip Salil, Adrienne Rich, Robert Bly and Ralph Russell. My acknowledgements are also due to the editors of literary e-journals: *Muse India*, *Kritya*, *Sketchbook* and Gene Doty's *Ghazal Page*, where some of these translations first appeared. I am also grateful to my niece Shiwangi, nephew Animesh and friend Suvvada Hari Krishna for helping me on the computer, and last but not the least, my wife Deepa for goading me to complete the work.

Sunil Uniyal
Ghaziabad, India
May 2014

Part I

1

Phir mujhe deed-e-tar yaad aayaa
Dil jigar tashnah-e-fariyaad aayaa

Dam liyaa thaa na qayaamat ne hanoz
Phir tiraa vaqt-e-safar yaad aayaa

Zindagi yoon bhee guzar hee jaatee
Kyoon tiraa raahguzar yaad aayaa

Kyaa hee rizvaan se larraai hogee
Ghar tiraa khuld men gar yaad aayaa

Koyee veeraanee see veeraanee hai
Dasht ko dekh ke ghar yaad aayaa

Maine Majnoon pa larrakpan men Asad
Sang uthaayaa thaa ki sar yaad aayaa

1

Those moist eyes have come to my mind once again
My heart and liver thirst for a lament again

Doomsday has yet to halt to take a breath
Though the moment of your journey is here again

I would have surely passed my life anyhow
Why has your alley crossed my mind again?

Will not the gatekeeper of Paradise quarrel
If I think of your abode there again?

What is this wilderness before my wilderness?
I imagine my home in a forest again

Whene'er my boyhood aimed a stone at Majnu, Asad,
I remembered my own head again and again !

Majnu: The crazy lover of Laila in the Arabic lore; his real name
was Qais.
Asad: Ghalib's first pen-name, meaning 'lion'.

2

Arz-e-niyaaz-e-ishq ke kaabil nahin rahaa
Jis dil pe naaz thaa mujhe vo dil nahin rahaa

Jaataa hoon daagh-e-hasrat-e-hasti liye huey
Hoon shammaa-kushtaa darkhur-e-mahfil nahin rahaa

Marne ki, ai dil, aur hi tadbeer kar ki main
Shaayaane-dasto-baazu-e-kaatil nahin rahaa

Dil se havaa-e-kisht-e-vafaa mit gayee ki vaan
Haasil, sivaay hasrat-e-haasil nahin rahaa

Bedaad-e-ishq se nahin dartaa magar Asad
Jis dil pe naaz thaa mujhe vo dil nahin rahaa.

2

Love entreaties I can't make any more
The heart I was once proud of, is no more

I walk out with the stains of desires on my heart,
I am a lamp extinguished, fit for mehfil no more

Think of some other way to court Death, O heart,
I won't die at the hands of Love any more

No hope I have to cultivate the field of passion,
Barring a wish, nothing remains now any more

Love's tyranny I don't fear at all, Asad,
But the heart I was proud of, is no more

3

Mahram naheen hai tu hee navaahaa-e-raaz kaa
Yaan varnaa jo hijaab hai pardaa hai saaz kaa

Rang-e-shikasth subah-e-bahaar-e-nazaaraa hai
Yah vaqt hai shiguftan-e-gulhaa-e-naaz kaa

Sarfah hai zabt-e-aah men meraa, vagarnah main
Tomaa hoon ek hee nafas-e-jaangudaaz kaa

Hain baski josh-e-baadah se sheeshe uchhal rahe
Har goshah-e-bisaat hai sar sheeshah baaz kaa

Taaraaj-e-kaavish-e-gham-e-hijraan huaa Asad
Seenah ki thaa dafeenah guharhaa-e-raaz kaa

3

The voice of His mystery is to you an alien thing
The veil that appears here, is His musical string

The dawn of springdays is pale in colour
It's time when roses of coquetry are blooming

I'll cling on to my sighs, otherwise
One single breath is enough to melt my being

The turbulence of wine makes the glass leap
The head of the juggler is on the carpet rolling

The grief of separation has dug my heart, Asad,
Of the secret diamonds, it had been burying

4

Zikr us pareevash kaa, aur phir bayaan apnaa
Ban gayaa raqeeb aakhir, thaa jo raazdaan apnaa

Mai vo kyaa bahot peete, bazm-e-ghair men, Yaarab
Aaj hee huaa manzoor unko imtihaan apnaa

Manzar ik bulandee par, aur ham banaa sakte
Arsh se idhar hotaa kaash ke makaan apnaa

De vo jis qadar zillat, ham hansee men taalenge
Baare aashnaa niklaa, unkaa paasbaan, apnaa

Dard-e-dil likhoon kab tak, jaaoon unko dikhlaa doon
Ungliyaan figaar apnee, khaamah khoonchakaan apnaa

Ham kahaan ke daanaa the, kis hunar men yaktaa the
Besabab huaa Ghalib, dushman aasmaan apnaa

4

The mention in my own style of that angelic beauty
Has turned my confidant into my adversary

Today she has decided to test herself
O Lord, she drinks too much in my rival's company

Sure, the pinnacle of success would have been mine
If close to the sky an abode was built for me

I am now friends with the keeper of her house
My rival's abuses I'll take sportingly

How long should I write about my heart's sorrow?
My fingers bruised, my pen shedding blood – I must let her see

What wisdom I had borne, what skill unique?
Ghalib, for no reason, the Heaven has turned against me

5

Yeh na thee hamaari kismet ki visaal-e-yaar hotaa
Agar aur jeete rahte yehi intizaar hotaa

Tere vaade pe jiye ham, to yah jaan jhoot jaanaa
Ki khushi se mar na jaate, agar etibaar hotaa

Koyi mire dil se poochhe, tire teere-neemkash ko,
Yah khalish kahaan se hoti jo jigar ke paar hotaa

Kahun kis se main ki kyaa hai, shabe-gham buri balaa hai
Mujhe kyaa buraa thaa marnaa, agar ek baar hotaa

Huey ham jo mar ke rusvaa, huey kyon na garke-dariyaa
Na kabhi janaazaa uthtaa, na kaheen mazaar hotaa

Use kaun dekh saktaa, ki yagaanah hai vo yaktaa
Jo dui ki boo bhi hotee to kaheen duchaar hotaa

Ye masaail-e-tasavvuf, yah tiraa bayaan Ghalib,
Tujhe ham valee samajhte, jo na baadahkhvaar hotaa.

26

5

A union with the Beloved was not in my fate
Had I lived longer, longer still would have been my wait

It is false if you think by your promise I've lived
I would have died of joy had I believed in it.

Let someone enquire from me about the arrow shot by you
All this pain I won't have felt if my heart it had pierced through

What to say? The night of parting is to me a gloom and curse,
Had death come to me just once, it won't have been any worse

I have suffered even in death, I wish I had drowned in a sea,
With no funeral procession and no grave built over me

Who can see Him? He is the One and One only,
Had there been a likeness, we would have met Him surely

Ghalib, your musings mystical and your expressions quaint,
If you weren't a wine-addict, you would have been a saint !

6

Na thaa kuchch, to Khudaa thaa,
kuchch na hotaa, to Khudaa hotaa
Duboyaa mujhko hone ne,
na hotaa main to kyaa hotaa

Huaa jab gham se yoon be-his,
to gham kyaa sar ke katne kaa
Na hotaa gar judaa tan se,
to zaanoo par dharaa hotaa

Huyi muddat ki Ghalib mar gayaa,
par yaad aataa hai
Vo har ik baat par kahnaa,
ki yoon hotaa to kyaa hotaa?

6

God was when there wasn't anything
Had there been nothing, God would have been
My being has been my undoing,
What difference it makes if I had not been?

My head has gone senseless with grief,
Why should I mourn its beheading?
If dismembered it were not,
On my knees it would be resting

Ghalib has passed an age ago,
But keeps coming to our thought
With such questions: If it was thus,
Then what it would have wrought?

7

Darkhure kahro gazab jab koyi hamsaa na huaa
Phir ghalat kyaa hai ki hamsaa koyi paidaa na huaa

Bandagee men bhee vo aazaad-o-khutbeen hain ki ham
Ulte phir aayen, dar-e-kaabah agar vaa na huaa

Sabko maqbool hai daavaa teri yaktaayi kaa
Roo-baroo koyi but-e-aaeenah seemaa na huaa

Seene kaa daagh hai vo naalah ki lab tak na gayaa
Khaaq kaa rizq hai vo qatrah ki dariyaa na huaa

Har bun-e-moo se, dam-e-zikr, na tapke khoonaab
Hamzah kaa kissah huaa, ishq kaa charchaa na huaa

Qatare men dazlah dikhaayi na de, aur zuzb men kul
Khel larrkon kaa huaa, deedah-e-beenaa na huaa

Thee khabar garm ki Ghalib ke urrenge purze
Dekhne ham bhee gaye the, pa tamaashaa na huaa

7

Slander and torture in love when none has borne like me
It's quite clear that in this world there's no one like me

I can't detach from myself even as I pray
If I find His shrine shut I will just turn away

You are the One and One only, is agreed by all and sundry
Even if You are mirrored in an icon, it'll reflect You poorly

The grievance not coming to lips, leaves on the heart a mark
of pain
The drop that doesn't reach the river, goes to sand all in vain

If your eyes don't let blood-tears, the story-teller will just fail,
It won't be a love story but only a Hamza tale

If universe in a speck, or sea in a drop, you can't see,
Then a playful kid you are, a grown up man you can't be

Ghalib would be torn to shreds, was hot in the air,
We too went to see the fun, but it wasn't there

❧   ❧   ❧

Hamza: Hero of a Persian romance; the chief feature of the story
being 'tilism' (magical illusion).

8

Balaa se hain ye jo pesh-e-nazar dar-o-deevaar
Nigaah-e-shauq ko hain, baal-o-par dar-o-deevaar

Vufoor-e-ashq ne kaashaane kaa kiyaa yah rang
Ki ho gaye mire deevaar-o-dar, dar-o-deevaar

Naheen hai saayah kli sunkar naved-e-maqdam-e-yaar
Gaye hain chand qadam peshtar, dar-o-deevaar

Huyi hai kis qadar arzaani-e-mai-e-jalvah
Ki mast hai mire kooche men har dar-o-deevaar

Jo hai tujhe sar-e-saudaa-e-intizaar to aa
Ki hain dukaan-e-mataa-e—nazar dar-o-deevaar

Hujoom-e-giriyah kaa saamaan kab kiyaa maine
Ki gir parre na mire paanv par, dar-o-deevar

Nazar men khatke hai bin tere ghar kee aabaadee
Hameshaa rote hain ham dekhkar dar-o-deevaar

Na kah kisee se, ki Ghalib naheen zamaane men
Hareef-e-raaz-e-muhabbat, magar dar-o-deevaar

8

Trouble bearing before my eyes are these doors and walls
For passion's gaze, feathers and wings are these doors and walls

The flood of tears from my eyes has inundated my house
Many more walls and doors are in these doors and walls

It's not their shadow, just the good news of Beloved's coming,
That forward a few steps are these doors and walls

Much abundant is, O God, the glory of Your wine,
In my lane ecstatic are even these doors and walls

Come, if you want to buy some goods from waiting,
You'll see them all displayed against these doors and walls

Provisions adequate I didn't make for lament
So that on my feet do not fall these doors and walls

All things at home prick my eyes in your absence
I always weep while gazing at these doors and walls

Don't tell anyone, Ghalib, that there's none in the world
Who can keep love secret, but for these doors and walls !

9

Laraztaa hai miraa dil zehmat-e-mehar-e-darakhshaan par
Main hoon vo katarah-e-shabnam, ki ho khaar-e-bayaabaan par

Fanaa taaleem-e-dars-e-bekhudee hoon, us zamaane se
Ki Majnoon laam alif likhtaa thaa deevaar-e-dabistaan par

Faraaghat kis qadar rahtee mujhe, tashveesh-e-marham se
Baham gar sulh karte paaraahaa-e-dil namakdaan par

Mujhe ab dekhkar abr-e-shafaq aaloodaa yaad aayaa
Ki furqat men tiree aatash barastee thee gulistaan par

Vazuz parvaaz-e-shauq-e-naaz, kyaa baaqee rahaa hogaa
Qayaamat ik havaa-e-tund hai khaak-e-shaheedaan par

Na larr naaseh se, Ghalib, kyaa huaa gar usne shiddat kee
Hamaaraa bhee to aakhir zor chaltaa hai gareebaan par

9

My heart shudders at the rise of Sun at dawn
I'm a dewdrop trembling on a cactus-thorn!

I've been taking my lessons in selflessness,
Since that age when Majnoon scribbled alphabets

Freed I'll be from the trouble of searching an ointment
If for a sprinkle of salt, my heart wounds nod in agreement

Now, the cloudlines glow at sunset in our union,
Recalling the fire that rained in the garden in separation

Except the flight of passion, what's there that would last?
On martyr's dust, the wind of Doomsday blows quite fast

Ghalib, why do you pick a fight with the preacher?
You can very well go after your own collar !

10

Kyon jal gayaa na taab-e-rukh-e-yaar dekhkar
Jaltaa hoon apnee taaqat-e-deedaar dekh kar

Aatashparast kahte hain ahl-e-jahaan mujhe
Sar garm-e-naalah-e-shararbaar dekh kar

Bik jaate hain ham aap mataa-e-sukhan ke saath
Lekin ayaar-e-taba-e-khareedaar dekh kar

In aablon se paanv ke ghabraa gayaa thaa main
Jee khush huaa hai raah ko purkhaar dekh kar

Girnee thee ham pa barq-e-tajallee na Toor par
Dete hain baadah zirf-e-kadahkhvaar dekh kar

Sar phorrnaa vo Ghalib-e-shoreedaa haal kaa
Yaad aa gayaa mujhe tiree deevaar dekh kar

10

Why has the glow of Beloved's face not burnt me?
My own guts to withstand it, I now envy

When they see me wail aloud with fiery complaints,
'Hey, fireworshipper !', is how the people hail me

Those who have the craving to buy our poems,
We poets sell ourselves to them only

Earlier blisters on my feet made me shudder,
But now the road, strewn with thorns, makes me happy

I wish the lightning had struck my head, not Mount Tur,
But then, the wine is poured for one with drinking capacity

A distraught Ghalib won't forget to break his head
Against the walls of your abode whenever comes he

Mt. Tur: The mountain in Sinai, on which Moses (Musa)
           experienced the presence of the Lord.

11

Ghar jab banaa liyaa tere dar par kahe bighair
Jaanegaa ab bhee too na miraa ghar kahe bighair

Kahte hain jab rahee na mujhe taaqat-e-sukhan
Jaanoon kisee ke dil kee main kyoonkar kahe bighair

Kaam us se aa parraa hai ki jiskaa jahaan men
Leve na koyi naam, sitamgar kahe bighair

Jee hee men kuchh naheen hai hamaare, vagarnah ham
Sar jaaye yaa rahe, na rahen par kahe bighair

Chhorroongaa main na us but-e-kaafir kaa poojnaa
Chhorre na khalq go mujhe, kaafir kahe bighair

Ghalib na kar huzoor men too baar baar arz
Zaahir hai teraa haal sab un par kahe bighair

11

When without your consent, at your door I'm residing,
Will you still from me, my address be enquiring?

They say that I have no power of expression,
The truth is I don't know what her heart is hiding.

I am rather compelled to seek the help of one
Whom everybody is as a 'tyrant' knowing

My heart is empty, or I would have spoken
Without any fear of my own beheading

Even if the whole world calls me a Kafir
That idol I would go on worshipping

If we don't mention 'wine' and 'wine-cup'
Talk about God and Truth will be nothing

Ghalib, before Him why plead again and again,
He well knows your plight without your saying

12

Laazim thaa ki dekho miraa rastaa koyi din aur
Tanhaa gaye kyoon? Ab raho tanhaa koyi din aur

Mit jaayegaa sar, gar tiraa patthar na ghisegaa
Hoon dar pa tire naasiyah farsaa koyi din aur

Aaye ho kal aur aaj hee kahte ho, ki jaaoon?
Maanaa, ki hameshaa naheen achchhaa, koyi din aur

Haan, ai falaq-e-peer, javaan thaa abhee Aarif,
Kyaa teraa bigarrtaa, jo na martaa koyi din aur

Tum maah-e-shab-e-chaar duhum the mire ghar ke
Phir kyoon na rahaa ghar kaa vo naqshah koyi din aur

Naadaan ho jo kahte ho ki kyoon jeete hain Ghalib
Kismat men hai marne kee tamannaa koyi din aur

12

You didn't consider it necessary to wait a few days more
Alone you went, now be alone, a few days more

The head will go if your stone doesn't wear off
Let me rub my forehead at your door a few days more

You came only yesterday, but want to leave today
If you can't stay forever, can't it be a few days more?

Arif was young, O wise Sky, what harm was yours,
If he had went on to live a few days more?

He was, indeed, the full-moon of my abode
Why couldn't his light remain a few days more?

A fool you are if you ask, why Ghalib goes on living?
It is his fate to long for death a few days more

Arif: Zain-ul-Abidin Khan 'Arif', nephew of Ghalib's wife; a
        budding poet whom Ghalib had adopted as his son; his early
        death evoked this sad ghazal.

13

Na gul-e-nagmah hoon, na pardah-e-saaz
Main hoon apnee shikast kee aavaaz

Too aur aaraaish-e-kham-e-kaakul
Main, aur andeshahaa-e-door-o-daraaz

Laaf-e-tamkeen, fareb-e-saadahdilee
Ham hain, aur raazhaa-e-seenahgudaaz

Hoon giriftaar-e-ulfat-e-saiyyaad
Varnah baaqee hai taaqat-e-parvaaz

Mujhko poochhaa to kuchh gazab na huaa
Main ghareeb aur too ghareebnavaaz

13

I am no musical tone, no song blossoming
I am just the sound of my own heart breaking

You are adorning your curls, deeply engrossed, but
I am looking farther to some far away thing

We boast to be wise, but this is a self-delusion
The secrets beneath our chest keep us melting

A bird you are, ensnared by fowler's love,
Have you still in your wings power uplifting?

You came asking for me – it's no surprise,
Helpless I' m, and you the one who's caring

14

Rukhe nigaar se hai soz-e-jaavidaani-e-shamma
Huee hai aatash-e-gul, aab-e-zindagaani-e-shamma

Zabaan-e-ahal-e-zabaan men, hai margh khaamoshee
Yah baat bazm men, raushan huee zabaani-e-shamma

Kare hai sirf-ba eemaa-e-sholah kissaa tamaam
Batarz-e-ahal-e-fanaa hai, fasaanah khvaani-e-shamma

Gham usko hasrat-e-parvaanah kaa hai, ai sholah,
Tire larazne se zaahir hai naatvaani-e-shamma

Tire khayaal se rooh ehtizaaz kartee hai
Bajalvah rezi-e-baad-o-ba parfishaani-e-shamma

44

14

The face of the Beloved is a candle eternally glowing
The fire of His rose is life-water giving

To the literary masters, death means silence –
The candle-flame highlights this in their gathering

The end of their tale is suggested by its flame
The candle reminds us of those no more living

The longing of the moth comes to nought, O flame,
The candle's remorse is seen in your quivering

The thought of the Beloved makes the soul dance,
As if a breeze of glory has a candle fluttering

15

Zakhm par chhirrken kahaan tiphlaane—beparvaa namak
Kyaa mazaa hotaa agar patthar men bhi hotaa namak

Garde raahe-yaar hai saamaane-naaze-zakhme-dil
Varnaa hotaa hai jahaan men kis kadar paidaa namak

Shor-e-jaulaan thaa kinaare-bahr par kiskaa ki aaj
Gard-e-saahil hai bazakhm-e-maujah-e-dariyaa namak

Daad detaa hai mere zakhme-jiggar ki vaah- vaah
Yaad kartaa hai mujhe, dekhe hai vo jis jaa namak

Chhorr kar jaanaa tan-e-majrooh-e-aashiq haif hai
Dil talab kartaa hai zakhm, aur maange hain aazaa namak

Yaad hain Ghalib mujhe vo din ki vajd-e-zauq men
Zakhm se girtaa to main palkon se chuntaa thaa namak

15

Where are all the carefree kids who on my wounds can spill salt?
What a pleasure it would be if their stones were of salt?

It is the dust of Beloved's path, it is the joy of the wounded heart,
Who knows in how much measure has this world created salt?

Whose cry was heard loud on the shore of the sea today?
The sand has evidence of the wounds of the waves full of salt

The friend breaks into applause when he sees my broken heart,
He recalls me to his mind wherever he sees some salt

To leave your love in a lurch, is it not, alas, a shame?
The heart now longs for a wound, and the limbs, a pinch of salt

I remember those days, Ghalib, when in mad ecstasy
For my wounds I'd pick, with my eyelashes, grains of salt !

16

*Jahaan teraa naqsh-e-kadam dekhte hain
Khiyaabaan -khiyaabaan iram dekhte hain*

*Dil-aashuftaghaan khaal-e-kunj-e-dahan ke,
Suvaidaa men sair-e-adam dekhte hain.*

*Tire sarv-qaamat se ik kadd-e-aadam,
Kayaamat ke fitne ko kam dekhte hain.*

*Tamaashaa kar ai mahv-e-aainah-daaree,
Tujhe kis tamannaa se ham dekhte hain.*

*Banaakar faqeeron kaa ham bhes, Ghalib,
Tamaashaa-e-ahl-e-karam dekhte hain.*

16

Wherever your footprints I see
An Eden garden there I see

In the dimples of your face
It's an illusion that I see

Even the Doomsday would be short
Before your stature, your majesty

Hey you, lost in front of the mirror !
With what longing I gaze at you, see

Ghalib, donned in mendicant's robes,
Farce of the merciful I see

17

Maane-e-dashtnavardee koyi tadbeer naheen
Ek chakkar hai mire paanv me zanjeer naheen

Shauq us dasht men daurraaye hai mujhko ki jahaan
Jaadah ghair az nigaah-e-deedah-e-tasveer naheen

Hasrat-e-lazzat-e-aazaar rahee jaatee hai
Jaadah-e-raah-e-vafaa, juz dam-e-shamsheer naheen

Ranj-e-naumeedi-e-jaaved, gavaaraa rahiyo
Khush hoon gar naalah zabooneekash-e-taaseer naheen

Ghalib apnaa yah akeedah hai, bakaul-e-Naasikh,
Aap be-bahr hain jo motqid-e-Meer naheen

17

Nothing can stop me from desert-wandering
The whirl round my feet is no chain clinging

Frenzy makes me run where nothing grows
Wherever my eyes go, a path is stretching

As the pain subsides, desire for it increases
The road to oblivion is through a sword moving

My hopelessness in love is eternal but tolerable
I am glad, my lament is no disgrace facing

Ghalib, I too agree with the view of Nasikh:
"If you have no faith in Mir , you aren't Self-knowing."

Nasikh: Sheikh Imam Baksh 'Nasikh' was a contemporary poet and
friend of Ghalib;
Mir: Mir Taqi Mir, Ghalib's renowned predecessor, who
composed the largest Divaan of ghazals in Urdu.

18

Vo firaaq aur vo visaal kahaan?
Vo shab-o-roz-o-maah-o-saal kahaan?

Fursat-e-kaar-o-baar—e-shauq kise?
Zauq-e-nazzaarah-e-zamaal kahaan?

Dil to dil, vo dimaagh bhi na rahaa,
Shor-e-saudaa-e-khatta-o-khaal kahaan?

Aisaa aasaan nahin lahoo ronaa,
Dil me taaqat, jigar men haal kahaan?

Hamse chhootaa qimaar-khaanah-e-ishq
Vaan jo jaayen girah men maal kahaan?

Fikr-e-duniyaa men sar khapaataa hoon,
Main kahaan aur yeh bawaal kahaan?

Muzmahil ho gaye quvaa Ghalib,
Vo anaasir men etidaal kahaan?

18

Where are those meetings and those partings now?
Where are those days and nights, months and years now?

Who has time to fall in love nowadays?
Where is delight in gazing at the Beauty now?

That heart is gone, that mind is no more too,
Where is imagination's revelry now?

The tears of blood are hard to weep,
Where's strength in the heart and liver now?

Love's gambling house is out of reach,
Where are pennies in my pocket now?

I'm troubled by the concerns of the world,
Where do I fit into this pell-mell now?

All powers, Ghalib, I have lost,
Where's in my elements harmony now?

19

Maze jahaan ke apnee nazar men khaaq naheen
Sivaaye khoone jigar so jigar men khaaq naheen

Magar ghubaar hue par, havaa urraa le jaaye
Vagarnah taab-o-tavaan, baal-o-par men khaaq naheen

Yah kis bihisht shamaail kee aamad aamad hai
Ki ghair-e-jalvah-e-gul rahguzar men khaaq naheen

Khayaal-e-jalvah-e-gul se kharaab hai maikash
Sharaabkhaane ke deevaar-o-dar men khaaq naheen

Huaa hoon ishq kee ghaaratgiree se sharmindah
Sivaaye hasrat-e-taameer, ghar men khaaq naheen

Hamaare sher hain ab sirf dillagee ke Asad
Khulaa ki faayadah arz-e-hunar men khaaq naheen

19

In my eyes, the pleasures of the world are nothing at all
In the liver, except for the blood, there's nothing at all

Perhaps the wind may blow me, when I turn into dust
Otherwise, my wings and feathers have no strength or guts

Who's here who comes like a heavenly beauty
A bed of tulips is now where the road was dusty

The mere thought of lilies has left some drunk
Else within these tavern-walls all is bunk

Ashamed I'm at the havoc my love has wrought
Except a wish to reconstruct, all is nought

Now, Asad, my verse remains an idle pastime
To no avail the skill of setting words to rhyme

20

Kee vafaa hamse to ghair usko jafaa kahte hain
Hoti aayi hai ki achchhon ko buraa kahte hain

Aaj ham apni parishaani-e-khaatir unse
Kahne jaate to hain, par dekhiye kyaa kahte hain.

Agle waqton ke hain ye log, inhe kuchh na kaho
Jo mai-o-naghmaa ko andoh-rubaa kahte hain

Dekhiye laatee hai us shokh ki nakhvat kyaa rang
Uski har baat pe ham naam-e-Khudaa kahte hain.

Vahshat -o-Sheftaa ab marsiyaa kahven shaayad,
Mar gayaa Ghalib-e-aashuftaa-navaa kahte hain.

20

When she shows her love to me, others say she is unfaithful
In the eyes of the world, the good are bad always

Today I go to meet her to tell her about my plight
But let me see how I'll say, what I have to say

Just ignore them – these people are living in the past
They think that wine and song will take their grief away

See, what that Beauty's pride has its effect on me
At each word she utters, 'O God, O God !' I say

Vahshat and Shefta may now recite their elegies
Ghalib with his tragic voice, seems to have passed away

Vahshat and Shefta: Ghulam Ali Khan 'Vahshat' and Nawab
Mustafa Khan 'Shefta' were poet-friends of Ghalib.

21

Hairaan hoon dil ko rovoon ki peetoon jigar ko mai
Maqdoor ho to saath rakhoon nauhaagar ko main

Chorraa na rashq ne ki tire ghar kaa naam loon
Har ik se poochhtaa hoon ki jaaoon kidhar ko main

Jaanaa parraa raqeeb ke dar par hazaar baar
Ai kaash, jaantaa na tiri rahguzar ko main

Chaltaa hoon thorree door har ik tezrau ke saath
Pahchaantaa naheen hoon abhee, raahbar ko main

Phir bekhudee men bhool gayaa raah-e-koo-e-yaar
Jaataa vagarnah ek din apnee khabar ko main

21

Should I cry my heart out or beat my chest - I am confused
If I could, to mourn for me, a servant sure I would've used

It's envy that prevents me from identifying your abode,
Rather I've been asking all to point to me the right road

My rival's door a thousand times I've been compelled to go
How much I wish that the way to your alley I didn't know

Some miles every swift walker I match stride for stride
But I've not yet found a person who can be my guide

In sheer absent-mindedness I've lost my Beloved's lane,
Otherwise, I would have indeed discovered myself again

22

Daayim parraa huaa tire dar par naheen hoon main
Khaak aisee zindagi pe ki patthar naheen hoon main

Kyoon gardish-e-mudaam se ghabraa na jaaye dil
Insaan hoon piyaal-o-saaghar naheen hoon main

Yaarab, zamaanaa mujhko mitaataa hai kis liye
Lauh-e-jahaan pa harf-e-muqar rar naheen hoon main

Kis vaaste azeez naheen jaante mujhe?
Laal-o-zamurood-o-zar-o-gauhar naheen main

Ghalib vazeefaa-khvaar ho, do Shaah ko duaa
Vo din gaye ki kahte the, naukar naheen hoon main

22

I wish I were forever lying at Your doorstep,
This life is dust, if no stone of Your pathway I am

Why won't my heart swirl in the whirls of adversity?
After all a human being, no wine or wine-cup, I am

O God, why is this world bent on erasing me?
No extra word written on its slate I am

Why isn't my worth known to my dear friends?
Neither a ruby, nor a pearl, nor gold, nor diamond I am

O Ghalib, bless the King, for you are on his roll,
Those days are past when you said, 'No servant I am.'

King(*Shah*): Reference is to Bahadur Shah Zafar, the last Mughal;
he had appointed Ghalib as his court-poet after the
death of Zauq.

23

Dono jahaan de ke vo samjhaa yeh khush rahaa
Yaan aa parree ye sharm ki taqraar kyaa Karen

Thak-thak ke har mukaam pe do-chaar rah gaye
Teraa pataa na paayen to naachaar kyaa Karen?

Kyaa shamma ke naheen hain havaakhvaah ahle bazm
Ho gham hee jaangudaaz to ghamkvaar kyaa Karen?

23

He gifted me both the worlds and thought I would be happy
But it has been such a shame that I could not disagree

Seekers get tired in Your quest, and at each turn some drop out
What else the poor ones can do, on not finding Your
whereabout?

Is the candle without its well-wishers in this gathering?
What good is their sympathy, if pain itself melts its being?

24

Sab kahaan, kuchh laal-o-gul men numaayaa ho gayeen
Khaaq men kyaa soorten hongi ki pinhaan ho gayeen

Theen banaatun-naash-e-gardu, din ko parde men nihaan
Shab ko unke jee men kyaa aayi ki uriyaan ho gayeen

Neend uski hai, dimaagh uskaa hai, raaten uski hain
Teri zulfen jiske baazoo par parishaan ho gayeen

Ham muvaahid hain, hamaaraa kesh hai tark-e—rusoom
Millaten jab mit gayeen, aj-zaa-e-imaan ho gayeen

Ranj se khoogar huaa insaan to mit jaataa hai ranj,
Mushkilen mujhpar parreen itnee ki aasaan ho gayeen

Yoon hi agar rotaa rahaa Ghalib, to ai ahal-e-jahaan,
Dekhnaa in bastiyon ko tum ki viraan ho gayeen

24

Few, very few are as roses or tulips returning
Who knows how many faces the dust has been covering?

The stars are hidden in the light of the day,
What happens at night, they come out all revealing.

His is the sleep and peace of mind, and his the night too,
On whose arms your hair you are spreading.

In the One we believe, but are not bound by rituals,
Creeds die when to faith they are converting

Hardships that poured on me were easily borne, for
Sorrow vanishes when one is used to suffering

O dwellers of the world, if Ghalib weeps well,
You'll see your cities into wilderness turning !

25

Dil hee to hai, na sang-o-khisht, dard se bhar na aaye kyoon?
Royenge ham hazaar baar, koyee hamen sataaye kyoon?

Dair naheen, haram naheen, dar naheen, aastaan naheen
Baithe hain rahguzar pa ham, koyee hamen uthaaye kyoon?

Qaid-e-hayaat-o-band-e-gham asl men dono ek hain
Maut se pahle, aadmee gham se nijaat paaye kyoon?

Haan vo naheen khudaaparast, jaao vo bevafaa sahee
Jisko ho deen-o-dil azeez, uskee galee men jaaye kyoon?

Ghalib-e-khastah ke bighair, kaun se kaam band hain?
Royeeye zaar zaar kyaa, keejiye haaye haaye kyoon?

25

It's my heart, no brick or stone, why won't it be filled with grief?
Why should someone torment me, when a thousand times I weep?

There's no temple, nor a mosque, neither a door nor a doorsill,
I am sitting by a road, why should I be asked to leave?

The prison of life and bonds of woe, are indeed one and the same,
How can a man before his death, from his suffering become free?

Yes, she has no fear of God and is utterly unfaithful
He who loves both Faith and Life, why should he enter her alley?

Without Ghalib, the ruined man, what work can come to halt?
If he's no more, for him why to weep bitterly?

26

Rahiye ab aisee jagah chalkar, jahaan koyee na ho
Hamsukhan koyee na ho, aur hamzabaan koyee na ho

Be daro-deevaar saa ik ghar banaanaa chaahiye
Koyee hamsaayaa na ho aur paasbaan koyee na ho

Parriye gar beemaar, to koyee na ho teemaardaar
Aur agar mar jaayiye to nauhaakhvaan koyee na ho

26

Let us go to live where nobody else is there
No one to speak to us, none knowing our tongue

Let us build a house there
Without any door or any wall
And let there be no neighbour
Nor servant at our beck and call

Let there be no one to nurse us if we fall ill
And if we die, none to sing the mourning-song

27

Kisi ko deke dil koyee navaa sanje phugaan kyoon ho?
Na ho jab dil hi seene men to phir munh men zabaan kyoon ho?

Vo apnee khoo na chhorrenge, ham apnee vaza kyoon badlen
Subuksar banke kyaa poochhen ki hamse sargiraan kyoon ho?

Kiyaa ghamkhvaar ne rusvaa, lage aag is muhabbat ko
Na laave tab jo gham kee, vo meraa raazdaan kyoon ho?

Qafas men mujhse roodaad-e-chaman kahte na dar, hamdam,
Giree hai jis pe kal bijlee vo meraa aashiyaan kyoon ho?

Yah fitnaa aadmee kee khaanah veeraanee ko kyaa kam hai
Huve tum dost jiske, dushman uskaa aasmaan kyoon ho?

Nikaalaa chaahtaa hai kaam kyaa taanon se too, Ghalib?
Tire be-mehr kahne se vo tujh par meherbaan kyoon ho?

27

When my heart I have surrendered, why should I utter cries of pain?
When the breast is without heart, why should the tongue in mouth remain?

If He cannot mend his ways, then why should we?
Why to be meek and ask, why He is angry?

That love I will destroy which brings bad name to me;
One who can't bear my grief, my friend can never be.

I am in a cage, O friend, tell me the garden's story;
The nest burnt by lightning, might not have belonged to me.

To ruin my house, it is enough - this torment, this calamity;
With you as a friend, I won't need the Heavens to be my enemy

Ghalib, why do you want your barbs to work for you?
When you say, she is unkind, how can kind she be?

28

Junoon tohmat kash-e-taskeen na ho, gar shaadmaanee kee
Namak paash-e-kharaash-e-dil hai, lazzat zindgaanee kee

Kashaakash haa-e-hastee se kare kyaa sai-e-aazaadee
Huyee zanjeer, mauj-e-aab ko fursat ravaanee kee

Pas az murdan bhee deevaanaa ziyaaratgaah-e-tiflaan hai
Sharaar-e-sang ne turbat pe meree gulfishaanee kee

28

Why blame my frenzy in love, if it seeks comfort in rejoicing
A pinch of salt on my heart sores is to my life's liking

Why should one try to free oneself from the travails of existence
The wave of water feels shackled when at ease it is flowing

He who has died mad in love, his grave is a pilgrimage for kids
Rose-like are sparks from stones, that on his tomb they are throwing

29

Aa ki mere jaan ko qaraar naheen hai
Taaqat-e-bedaad-e-intizaar naheen hai

Dete hain jannat hayaat-e-dahr ke badle
Nashah ba-andaaz-e-khumaar naheen hai

Giriyah nikaale hai tiri bazm se mujhko
Haay! ki rone pa ikhtiyaar naheen hai

Dil se uthaa lutf-e-jalwahaah-e-ma-aanee
Ghair-e-gul, aainaa-e-bahaar naheen hai

Toone qasam maikashee kee khayee hai Ghalib
Teri qasam kaa kuchh aitibaar naheen hai

29

Come, Beloved, no peace I'm having
I can't endure anymore this waiting

The gift of heaven in lieu of this life
Is a hangover after all drinking

Tears force me out of your party
I regret, I cannot control my weeping

If the heart's without joy, there's no meaning
If the rose doesn't bloom, there's no spring

Ghalib, you've taken an oath against drinking,
But nobody is sure that you'll be keeping!

30

Har qadam doori-e-manzil hai numaayaan mujhse
Meree raftaar se aage hai bayaabaan mujhse

Vahshat —e-aatash-e-dil se shab-e-tanhaai men,
Soorat-e-dood rahaa saayaa gurezaan mujhse

Asar-e-aablah se, jaadah-e-sahraa-e-junoon
Soorat-e-rishtah-e-gauhar hai charaaghaan mujhse

Nigah-e-garm se ik aag tapaktee hai, Asad,
Hai charaaghaan, khas-o-khaashaak-e-gulistaan mujhse

30

At every step, my goal goes farther
I run fast, but the desert runs faster

In the night of loneliness, it is my grief that burns
While like a ring of smoke, from me my shadow turns

Blisters on my feet have left a bloody imprint
Shimmering in my desert, like a pearl-string

From my hot eyes, Asad, a fire is dripping
In which even the dry leaves of my garden are burning

31

Ek jaa harf-e-vafaa likkhaa thaa so bhee mit gayaa
Zaahiraa kaaghaz tire khat kaa ghalat bardaar hai

Jee jale zauq-e-fanaa kee naatmaamee par na kyoon
Ham naheen jalte, nafas harchand aatashbaar hai

Aag se paanee men bujhte vaqt uthtee hai sadaa
Har koyi darmaandagee men naale se naachaar hai

Hai vahee badmasti-e-har zarre kaa khud uzrakhvaah
Jiske jalve se zameen taa aasmaan sarshaar hai

Mujhse mat kah, too hame kahtaa thaa apnee zindagee
Zindagee se bhee miraa jee in dino bezaar hai

Aankh kee tasveer sarnaame pe khenchee hai ki taa
Tujh pe khul jaave, ki usko hasrat-e-deedaar hai

31

The word 'love' in your letter has proved to be false
The paper itself is in the act of erasing

Why won't my heart burn if the wish for oblivion remains?
But I won't merge in dust, my breath with love is sparkling

The fire cries out when doused with water :
When in distress, one can't help lamenting

Lord's glory intoxicates every sand grain
At His will earth and sky are revolving

Don't say to me that 'You are my life'
Life itself to my Self is now boring

On the envelope I've drawn an eye's sketch
It is clear, for your sight I'm longing

32

Shabnam ba gul-e-laalah na khaali zi adaa hai
Daagh-e-dil-e-bedard nazargaah-e-hayaa hai

Shole se na hoti, havas-e-sholah ne jo kee
Jee jis qadar afsurdagi-e-dil pa jalaa hai

Qumree kaf-e-khaakistar-o-bulbul qafas-e-rang
Ai naalah nishaan-e-jigar-e-sokhtah kyaa hai

Majboori-o-daavaa-e-giriftaari-e-ulfat
Dast-e-tah-e-sang aamadah paimaan-e-vafaa hai

Ai partab-e-khursheed-e-jahaantaab idhar bhee
Saaye kee tarah ham pa ajab vaqt parraa hai

Begaangee-e-khalq se bedil na ho, Ghalib,
Koyee naheen teraa, to miri jaan Khudaa hai

32

The tear-drop on a poppy has, indeed, some meaning
The cruel heart knows how its shame it is concealing

Stronger than fire itself, is the longing for fire
The spirit of heart gets burnt out with suffering

The dove is charred, while the caged nightingale shrieks
Before their cries, my own lament means nothing

It is compulsion that makes one prisoner of love
The hand is faithful when 'neath a boulder it is coming

O Sun, O World Illuminator, emit your beams,
Time's strange shadow is upon us descending

Ghalib, don't be disheartened by world's apathy
God is there, even if none is forthcoming

33

Miri hastee fazaa-e-hairat aabaad-e-tamannaa hai
Jise kahte hain naalah vo isee aalam kaa anqaa hai

Khazaan kyaa? fasl-e-gul kahte hain kisko?koyi mausam ho
Vahee ham hain, qafas hai, aur maatam baal-o-par kaa hai

Vafaa-e-dilbaraan hai ittifaaqee, varnah ai hamdam!
Asar fariyaad-e-dilhaa-e-hazeen kaa, kisne dekhaa hai?

Na laayee shokhi-e-andeshah taab-e-ranj-e-naumeedee
Kaf-e-afsos malnaa, ahad-e-tajdeed-e-tamannaa hai

33

An open expanse of amazement, full of longing, is my existence
Where the lament of my heart is like a voiceless bird's presence

When is autumn? When is spring? I don't know
A caged nightingale bereft of wings – my life is so

It's sheer chance that the one who steals your heart, is faithful, too,
Otherwise one's sighing or complaining in love never comes true

The thought of your mischievousness, in my grief, no solace brings
When I vow to renew my longing, the hand of regret wrings !

34

Muddat huvee hai yaar ko mehmaan kiye huve
Josh-e-qadah se bazm charaaghaan kiye huve

Phir garm-e-naalah haa-e-shararbaar hai nafas
Muddat huvee hai sair-e-charaaghaan kiye huve

Baaham digar huve haibn dil-o-deedah phir raqeeb
Nazzaarah-o-khayaal kaa saamaan kiye huve

Maage hai phir kisee ko lab-e-baam par havas
Zilf-e-siyaah rukh pa pareeshaan kiye huve

Jee dhoondhtaa hai phir vahee fursat ke raat din
Baithe rahen tasavvur-e-jaanaan kiye huve

Ghalib hame na chherr ki phir josh-e-ashk se
Baithe hain ham tahayyah-e-toofaan kiye huve

34

An age has passed since I hosted my Beloved
When our evenings were lit up with cups of wine

My breath is hot again with fiery complaints,
It's long since we saw the fireworks shine

The heart and the eyes, arch rivals though,
Together for Beloved's sight they now pine

Again I wish my Love's on her balcony,
With dark tresses blowing on her face fine

The heart again seeks those days and nights of leisure
When in thoughts I would with my Beloved entwine

Ghalib, don't provoke me, for I'm ready again
With my turbulent tears to let a stormy rain !

35

Koyi ummeed bar naheen aatee
Koyi soorat nazar naheen aatee

Maut kaa ek din muayyan hai
Neend kyoon raat bhar naheen aatee?

Aage aatee thee haal-e-dil pa haseen
Ab kisee baat par naheen aatee

Jaantaa hoon savaab-e-taayat-o-zohad
Par tabeeyat idhar naheen aatee

Hai kuchh aisee hi baat, jo chup hoon
Varnah kyaa baat kar naheen aatee

Daagh-e-dil gar nazar naheen aataa
Boo bhee ai chaaraaghar naheen aatee?

Ham vahaan hain jahaan se hamko bhee
Kuchh hamaaree khabar naheen aatee

Marte hain aarzoo men marne kee
Maut aatee hai par naheen aatee

Kaabah kis munh se jaaoge Ghalib?
Sharm tumko magar naheen aatee

35

My hopes bear no fruit anymore
I see no prospect anymore

Death is bound to come one day,
Why can't I sleep at night anymore?

Earlier I laughed at my own heart,
Nothing now makes me laugh anymore

I know the ascetic way is good
But I've no fondness for it anymore

Some reason is sure, why I'm quiet
Don't think, I can't speak anymore

If you can't see my heart's scar,
Healer, can't you smell it anymore?

Now I am in such a plight that
I'm not aware of myself anymore

I'm dying in anticipation of death,
It comes, yet not comes anymore

What face you'll go Kaaba, Ghalib?
You bear no sense of shame anymore

36

Dil-e-naadaan tujhe huaa kyaa hai?
Aakhir is dard kee davaa kyaa hai?

Ham hain mushtaaq aur vo bezaar,
Yaa Ilaahee, yah maajraa kyaa hai?

Main bhee munh men zabaan rakhtaa hoon
Kaash, poochho ki mudduaa kyaa hai?

Jab ki tum bin naheen koyi maujood,
Phir yah hamgaamah ai Khudaa, kyaa hai?

Hamko unse vafaa kee hai ummeed
Jo naheen jaante, vafaa kyaa hai?

Haan bhalaa kar, tiraa bhalaa hogaa
Aur darvesh kee sadaa kyaa hai?

Jaan tum par nisaar kartaa hoon,
Main naheen jaantaa, duaa kyaa hai?

Mane maanaa ki kuchh naheen Ghalib,
Muft haath aaye, to buraa kyaa hai?

36

O naive heart, what the matter is?
For this pain, what the cure is?

I am anxious but she's distraught
O Lord, what the issue is?

I too have a tongue in my mouth
Ask, what my intent is?

When nothing exists without You
O God, then why this hubbub is?

We expect loyalty from those
Who don't know what loyalty is

'Do good, and good will come to you'
What else the mendicant's call is?

I am offering my life to you,
I know not what your blessing is

A thing is nothing at all, Ghalib,
But why curse it, if free it is?

37

Har ek baat pe kahte ho tum ki tu kyaa hai?
Tumhin kaho ki yah andaaz-e-guftagoo kyaa hai?

Na shole men yah karishmaa, na barq men yah adaa,
Koyi bataao ki vo shokh-e-tundkhoo kyaa hai?

Jalaa hai jism jahaan dil bhee jal gayaa hogaa,
Kuredte ho jo ab raakh, zustjoo kyaa hai?

Ragon men daurrne phirne ke ham naheen qaayal
Jab aankh hee se na tapkaa, to phir lahoo kyaa hai?

Vo cheez, jiske liye hamko ho, bihisht azeez
Sivaay baadah-e-gulfaam-e-mushkaboo kyaa hai?

Rahee na taaqat-e-guftaar aur agar ho bhee
To kis umeed pa kahiyeki aarzoo kyaa hai?

Huaa hai Shah kaa musaahib, phire hai itraataa,
Vagarnah shahar men Ghalib kee aabroo kyaa hai?

37

Whenever I say something, you say 'Who are you?'
Tell me, the way you speak, does it behove you?

There's no miracle in the flame, nor style in lightning
Let somebody tell me what that petulant one is possessing

When the body has burnt, the heart has burnt, too,
It is all ash-heap now, what's there to dig into?

The blood that just runs in the veins, is no blood
If from eyes it doesn't drip, it doesn't shed

The Paradise is dear to me for just one thing:
The promise of wine - rosy and musk-smelling

I've lost my power of speech, but even if it was with me
On what hope I would have expressed my wish to Thee?

He shows off walking around, for he is now a friend of the King,
Otherwise, in this city, for his honour Ghalib has nothing

38

*Ibn-e-Mariyam huaa kare koyi
Mere dukh ki davaa kare koyi.*

*Baat par vaan zubaan kat tee hai
Vo kahen aur sunaa kare koyi*

*Bak rahaa hoon junoon men kyaa kyaa
Kuchh na samjhe Khudaa kare koyi*

*Rok lo gar ghalat chale koyi
Bakhsh do gar khataa kare koyi*

*Kyaa kiyaa Khizr ne Sikandar se,
Ab kise rahnumaa kare koyi?*

*Jab tavakko hi uth gayi Ghalib
Kyon kisi kaa gilaa kare koyi?*

38

Like Mary's Son, may someone be
Of all my pain, may He cure me

You speak – your tongue would be slit,
She talks – a listener you should be

What in madness I'm uttering?
O God, I wish none understands me

Stop him from doing a wrong thing,
Forgive, if an error commits he

The Khizr couldn't guide Sikandar,
Who can show the way to me?

Ghalib, when all our hope is gone,
Complaining still why are we?

Khizr: In Islamic tradition, Khizr and Sikandar (i.e. Alexander
         the Great) are said to have gone to seek the Fountain of
         Life, but Khizr alone discovered it, and tasting the divine
         elixir, became immortal; he is ever living and guides the
         lost travellers.

39

Us bazm men mujhe naheen bantaa hayaa kiye
Baithaa rahaa, agarche ishaare huaa kiye

Rakhtaa phiroon hoon khirkah-o-sajjadah rahan-e-mai
Muddat huyi hai daavat-e-aab-o-havaa kiye

Maqdoor ho to khaaq se poochoon ki ai laeem
Toone vo ganjhaa-e-giraanmaayah kyaa kiye?

Sohbat men ghair kee na parree to kaheen yah khoo
Dene lagaa hai bosaa bighar iltijaa kiye

Zid kee hai aur baat, magar khoo buree naheen
Bhoole se usne saikaron vaade vafaa kiye

Ghalib tumhee kaho ki milegaa javaab kyaa?
Maanaa ki tum kahaa kiye, aur vo sunaa kiye

39

In your assembly my self-esteem has no clout
But even if fingers point at me, I won't go out

I've pawned my robes and prayer-rug for your wine
Though I can't tell when at last we drank and dined

If I could, I would have asked the Mother Earth:
Why a miser you have been in doling your treasure?

She has taken from my rival this new habit –
Of planting a kiss even before I beg for it

Though stubborn, she is never misbehaving
Though forgetful, many a promise she's keeping

What answers you'll get Ghalib, please tell me
When to your babble, just a listener is she

40

Baazeechaa-e-atfaal hai duniyaa, mire aage
Hotaa hai shab-o-roz tamaashaa, mire aage.

Ik khel hai aurang-e-Sulaimaan mire nazdeek
Ik baat hai aizaaz-e-Maseehaa, mire aage

Juz naam nahin soorte-aalam mujhe manjoor
Juz vaham nahin hasti-e-ashiyaa, mire aage

Hotaa hai nihaan gard men sahraa mire hote
Ghistaa hai zabeen khaaq pe dariyaa, mire aage

Mat poochh ki kyaa haal hai meraa, tire peechhe
Tu dekh ki kyaa rang hai teraa, mire aage

Sach kahte ho, khudbeeno-khud-aaraa na kyon hoon
Baithaa hai bute-aainaa —seemaa, mire aage

Phir dekhiye andaaze-gul afshaani-e-guftaar
Rakh de koyi paimaanaa-o-sahbaa, mire aage

40

This world is a kids' playground to me,
Day and night a sport goes on before me

The throne of Solomon is just an amusement,
In the miracle of Christ, an anecdote I see

I don't accept that the world is real,
It's just a name, an illusion before me

At my plight the desert covers itself with sand
And the river rubs its forehead on the mud before me

Don't ask me how I feel in your absence,
I see that you yourself go pale on seeing me

You are right in thinking that I'm thinking of myself,
For, a mirror-like Beauty sits in front of me

You will yourself see how the gossip flows,
If a jar filled with wine is placed before me

Nafrat kaa gumaan guzre hai, main rashq se guzraa
Kyonkar kahoon, lo naam na unkaa, mire aage

Imaan mujhe roke hai, to kheenche hai mujhe kufr
Kaabaa mire peechhe hai, kaleesaa, mire aage

Khush hote hain par vasl men yoon mar nahin jaate
Aayi shab-e-hijraan kee tamannaa, mire aage

Hai maujzan ik qulzum-e-khoon, kaash yahee ho,
Aataa hai abhi dekhiye kyaa-kyaa, mire aage

Go haath ko jumbish naheen, aankhon me to dam hai,
Rahne do abhee saagar-o-meenaa, mire aage

Ham-peshaa-o-ham-mashrab-o -hamraaz hai meraa
Ghalib ko buraa kyoon kaho, achchhaa mire aage.

I don't want you to take her name in my presence,
There's no rancour, just envy within me

The idol attracts but Faith comes to my rescue,
The Kaaba is behind me, the church in front of me

The meeting time is all bliss, with no feeling of Death,
Yet in it the thought of parting hassles me

All around me a sea of blood surges,
It's okay, if not, what worse there can be?

My hands can't move but my eyes still glisten,
I wish the cup of wine stays before me

He shares the same vocation, same creed, same secrets,
Then why you call Ghalib, 'bad' before me?

41

Bahot sahee gham-e- getee, sharaab kam kyaa hai
Ghulaam-e-saaqi-e-Kausar hoon, mujhko gham kyaa hai?

Tumhaaree tarz-o-ravish, jaante hain ham, kyaa hai
Raqeeb par hai agar lutf, to sitam kyaa hai?

Sukhan men khaamah-e-Ghalib kee aatash afshaanee
Yaqeen hai hamko bhee, lekin ab usme dam kyaa hai?

41

The world is full of sorrow, but where's the dearth of wine?
I serve the King's cup-bearer, how can the grief be mine?

Your style, your behaviour – I know what it is
You've graced my rival - what else cruelty is?

In verses, the fireworks of Ghalib's pen –
We too believe, but now what's left in them?

42

Kunj men baithaa rahoon, yoon par khulaa
Kaash ke hotaa qafas kaa dar khulaa.

Ham pukaare aur khule, yoon kaun jaaye?
Yaar kaa darvaazaa paayen garm khulaa.

Hamko hai is raazdaaree par ghamand
Dost kaa hai raaz dushman par khulaa.

Vaaqai dil par bhalaa lagtaa thaa daagh
Zakhm lekin daagh se behtar khulaa.

Muft kaa kisko buraa hai Badraqah
Rahravee men pardah-e-rahbar khulaa.

Soz-e-dil kaa kyaa kare baaraan-e-ashk?
Aag bharrkee meh agar dam bhar khulaa.

Naame ke saath aa gayaa paighaam-e-margh
Rah gayaa khat meri chhaatee par khulaa.

Dekhiyo Ghalib se gar uljhaa koyi,
Hai valee posheedah, aur kaafir khulaa.

❧   ❧   ❧

42

I wish I was resting free in a garden,
If only the gate of my cage was open

I call, it opens: who'll enter like that
If the door of my beloved is open

I am taking pride in this mystery:
To my foe, my friend's secret is open

The scar looks good on my heart
It were better if the wound was open

What harm if you have a free Guide?
Walk with Him, His veil will open

What the tears do to a grieving heart?
If they cease raining, the fire will open

The mail brought news of a friend's passing,
The letter on my chest lay open

Beware to pick an argument with Ghalib,
He's a hidden saint, but an infidel open

Part II

43

Havas ko hai nishaat-e-kaar kyaa kyaa
Na ho marnaa to jeene kaa mazaa kyaa?

Tajaahul peshgee se mudduaa kyaa?
Kahaan tak ai saraapaa naaz, kyaa kyaa?

Farog-e-sholah-e-khas yaq nafas hai
Havas ko paas-e-naamoos-e-vafaa kyaa?

Nafas mauj-e-muheet-e-bekhudee hai
Taghaaful haa-e-saaqee kaa gilaa kyaa?

Dil-e-har qatarah hai saaz-e-analbahar,
Ham uske hain hamaaraa poochhnaa kyaa?

Balaa-e-jaan hai Ghalib uskee har baat,
Ibaarat kyaa, ishaarat kyaa, adaa kyaa?

43

From desire many joys of action spring,
If there's no death, will we relish life?

How long you'll feign ignorance?
How long your coquettishness say, 'What, what?'

The straw aflame shines for a single breath,
What respect passion has for the sanctity of faithfulness?

My breath is like a wave in a sea of selflessness,
Why to blame the cupbearer for her negligence?

The heart of every drop sings, "I'm the sea",
We belong to Him, why seek answers from us?

Ghalib, whatever the Beloved bestows,
Is a catastrophe - be it speech, or gesture, or grace

44

Ghar hamaaraa jo na rote bhee to veeraan hotaa
Bahr gar bahr na hotaa, to bayaabaan hotaa

Tangi-e-dil kaa gilaa kyaa, yah vo kaafir dil hai
Ki agar tang na hotaa, to pareeshaan hotaa

Baad-e-yak umra-e-bara, baar to detaa baare
Kaash rizvaan hee dar-e-yaar kaa darbaan hotaa

44

My house would have been a wilderness even if I had not shed tears
If the ocean was not an ocean, it would still have been a desert

About my heart's narrowness, what complaint should I make?
A kafir it is, if not narrow, it would still be much confused

If I bore patience all my life, Heaven's Doorkeeper would let me in
I wish my Beloved's doorkeeper could have imbibed that culture

45

Huee taakheer to kuchh baais-e-taakheer bhee thaa
Aap aate the, magar koi inaangeer bhee thaa

Tumse bejaa, hai mujhe apnee tabaahee kaa gilaa
Isme kuchh shaayabah-e-khoobi-e-taqdeer bhee thaa

Tu mujhe bhool gayaa ho to pataa batlaa doon
Kabhee fitraak men tere koi nakhcheer bhee thaa

Qaid men hai tire vahshee ko vahee zulf kee yaad
Haan kuchh ik ranj-e-garaanbaari-e-zanjeer bhee thaa

Bijlee ik kaund gayi aankhon ke aage to kyaa?
Baat karte, ki main lab tashnah-e-taqreer bhee thaa

Rekhte ke tumheen ustaad nahin ho Ghalib
Kahte hain agle zamaane men koi Meer bhee thaa

45

You are late - for this delay, there must be a reason sure
Tell me, was there someone who waylaid you?

To blame you wholly for my ruin is not just,
Perhaps, my good fate should take some credit, too

If you've forgotten me, I'll remind you who I am –
Was I not a prey in your saddle-straps once?

Imprisoned is this madman in the memory of your curls
The painful burden of a chain is also felt by him

You gave me a lightning glimpse, then what?
I wish you had also conversed with my thirsty lips

You aren't the only master of Urdu, Ghalib,
It is said, in age goneby, there was a Mir, too

46

Dard minnat-e-kash davaa na huaa
Main na achchhaa huaa, buraa na huaa

Jamaa karte ho kyoon raqeebon ko?
Ik tamaashaa huaa, gilaa na huaa

Ham kahaan kismet aazmaane jaayen?
Too hee jab khanjar –aazmaan na huaa

Kitne sheereen hain tere lab, ki raqeeb
Gaaliyaan khaa ke bemazaa na huaa

Hai khabar garm unke aane kee
Aaj hee ghar men boriyaa na huaa

Kyaa vo Namrood kee khudaayi thee?
Bandagee men miraa bhalaa na huaa

Jaan dee, dee huee useekee thee
Haq to yah hai, ki haq adaa na huaa

Kuchh to parhiye ki log kahte hain
Aaj Ghalib ghazalsaraa na huaa

46

My suffering has no panacea
My condition's neither better nor worse

Friend, why do you gather my opponents?
To make fun of my grievance?

I'll have my luck tested only
If you throw the dagger at me

Your lips are honey - even my rival
Loves the abuses you hurl at me

I hear a guest is visiting today,
But there's no bedding in my house

My worship has done me no good -
Did I bow before a false god?

He gave me life and I offered it back to Him:
What's so special in giving what was His alone?

Friend, recite anything today
Ghalib isn't there to sing his ghazal

47

Aah ko chaahiye ik umra asar hone tak
Kaun jeetaa hai teri zulf ke sar hone tak

Daam-e-har mauj men haiHalqah-e-sadkaam nihang
Dekhen kyaa guzre hai qatare pa guhar hone tak

Aashiqee sabr talab, aur tamannaa betaab
Dil kaa kyaa rang karoon, khoon-e-jigar hone tak

Hamne maanaa ki taghaaful na karoge lekin
Khaak ho jaayenge ham, tumko khabar hone tak

Yak nazar bash naheen fursat-e-hastee ghaafil
Garmi-e-bazm hai, ik raqs-e-sharar hone tak

Gham-e-hastee kaa, Asad kis se ho juz margh ilaaj
Shamma har rang men jaltee hai sahar hone tak

47

My sigh will need a lifetime indeed to have its effect
Who'll live long to be conquered by the tassels of your hair?

Each wave lunges like a crocodile with a hundred jaws,
Each drop bears many risks before turning into a pearl

Love needs to be patient, but the desire is impatient,
What would be my heart's colour when it runs dry of blood?

I have faith that to me you'll not be indifferent
But by the time you are aware, I'd merge into dust

This life doesn't know whether it is there next moment;
The warmth of worldly gathering is a dance of bonfire

Asad, the woes of life have their cure only in death;
The candle burns out all its hues till the break of dawn

48

Gham naheen hotaa hai aazaadon ko vesh az yak nafas
Barq se karte hain roshan, shamma-e-maatamkhaanaa ham

Mahfilen barham kare hai ganjafaabaaz-e-khayaal
Hai varaq gardaani-e-nairang-e-yak butkhaanaa ham

Baavujood-e-yak jahaan hangaamaa paidaayee naheen
Hain charaaghaan-e-shabistaan-e-dil-e-parvaanaa ham

Zof se hai, na qanaa-at se, yah tark-e-justjoo
Hain vabaal-e-takiyaagaah-e-himmat-e-mardaanaa ham

Daayim-ul -habs isme hain laakhon tamannaayen Asad
Jaante hain seenah-e-purkhoo ko zindaan-khaanaa ham

48

Grief with we liberated ones, doesn't stay for more than a breath
It's with a lightning flash we kindle lamps in our mourning
chamber

Thought plays its cards so well that the gathering gets confused
We keep on turning the pages of the mysteries of His shrine

All this worldly hullabaloo, doesn't result in creativity,
We with restless hearts are like moths before a lamp

We have gone too weak to continue with our quest
Our spirit, woe-burdened, now seeks a place to rest

Millions of my cravings have been sentenced to life,
Asad, my heart is now a dungeon filled with blood

49

Meherbaan hoke bulaa lo mujhe chaaho jis vaqt
Main gayaa vaqt naheen hoon ki phir aa bhee na sakoon

Zof men taanah-e-aghyaar kaa shikvah kyaa hai
Baat kuchh sar to naheen hai, ki uthaa bhee na sakoon

Zahar miltaa hee nahin mujhko, sitamgar varnah
Kyaa qasam hai tire milne kee, ki khaa bhee na sakoon

49

Be kind to call me anytime that you please
I'm not like time gone by that I won't return

I'm too frail to grumble against my rival's taunt
It's not heavier than the head that I carry

O cruel one, there is no poison I can procure
Else, how the vow of meeting you, could I've taken ?

50

Kal ke liye kar aaj na khissat sharaab men
Yah soo-e-jan hai saaki-e-kausar ke baab men

Rau men hai rakhshe-umra, kahaan dekhiye thame
Na haath baag par hai, na paa rakaab men

Itnaa hi mujhko apni haqiqat se bod hai
Jitnaa ki vahme-ghair se hoon pech-o-taab men

Hai mushtamil numood-e-suvarpar vujood-e-bahar
Yaan kyaa dharaa hai qatra-e-mauj-o-habaab men

Aaraaish-e-jamaal se faarigh nahin hanoz
Pesh-e-nazar hai aainah daaim niqaab men

Hain ghaib-e-ghaib jisko samajte hain ham shuhood
Hain khvaab men hanoz, jo jaage hain khvaab men

Ghalib nadeem-e-dost se aatee hai boo-e-dost
Mashghool-e-haq hoon, bandagi-e-booturaab men

50

For your tomorrow, don't skip your drink today,
The cup-bearer of Paradise will feel disgraced

Life's stallion gallops ahead, where it'll halt, who can predict
No more the reins are in my hands, nor are stirrups on my feet

I am at a distance far removed from my own reality,
As much as the confusion created by the Unknown

The ocean is an ocean when it is a whole,
Not when it breaks into drops and waves

She's not satisfied with her make-up:
She's gazing at a mirror within her veil

What we see remains beyond our mind,
We are in a dream even when we are awake

From the friend's friend, Ghalib,
Comes a friendly fragrance – as if from God !

51

Gham-e-duniyaa se, gar payee thee fursat, sar uthaane kee
Falak kaa dekhnaa, taqreeb, tere yaad aane kee

Khulegaa kis tarah mazmoon mire maqtoob kaa yaarab
Qasam khaayi hai us kaafir ne kaaghaz ke jalaane kee

Lipatnaa parniyaan men sholah-e-aatash kaa aasaan hai
Vale mushkil hai hikmat, dil men soz-e-gham chhupaane kee

Unhen manjoor apne jakhmiyon kaa dekh aanaa thaa
Uthe the sair-e-gul ko, dekhnaa shokhee bahaane kee

Hamaaree saadgee thee, iltifaat-e-naaz par marnaa
Tiraa aanaa na thaa, Zaalim, magar tamheed jaane kee

Lakadkob-e-havaadis kaa tahammul kar nahin saktee
Miri taaqat, ki zaamin thee buton ke naaz uthaane kee

Kahoon kyaa khoobi-e-auzaa-e-ibnaa-e-zamaan Ghalib
Badee kee usne, jis se kee thee hamne baarahaa nekee

51

If I had time to lift my head from the woes of the world
A look at the sky would have reminded me of You, O Lord!

How can the contents of my letter be revealed,
That non-believer has already sworn to set it on fire

Easy it is to wrap in silk a piece of burning coal
But hard it is to hide the grief that burns the heart

She had promised to care for the wounded ones,
Look at her mischief – she strolls in a rose-garden!

It was naive of me to be carried away by her kind words,
Her coming was no coming, but just a prelude to leaving

No longer can I bear the blows and butts of misfortune
I'm too weak to endure the coquetry of idols now

Ghalib, I can't vouch for the 'goodness' of my friends
Whomsoever I helped, has turned his back on me

52

Kyaa tang ham sitam zadgaan kaa jahaan hai
Jisme ki ek baiz-e-mor aasmaan hai

Hai qaainaat ko harkat tere zauq se
Partau se aaftaab ke zarre men jaan hai

Haalaanki hai yah seli-e-khaaraa se laal rang
Ghaafil ko mere sheeshee pe main kaa gumaan hai

Baithaa hai jo ki saayah-e-deevaar-e-yaar men
Farmaanravaa-e-kishvar-e-Hindostaan hai

Hai baare, aitimaad-e-vafaadaaree is qadar
Ghalib ham isme khush hain, ki naa mehrbaan hai

52

The world of we distressed ones, is too narrow
The sky over us is an ant's egg

The sand grains dance when lit by Your Sun
Who makes the world go round, but You?

The tulip turns red when struck by a stone
The ignorant think my glass holds wine

He who sits in the shade of Beloved's wall,
Is, indeed, like the Emperor of Hindustan

So much we trust our Beloved, Ghalib,
That we are happy even when He is unkind!

53

Masjid ke zer-e-saayah kharaabaat chaahiye
Bhaun paas aankh, qiblah-e-haajaat chaahiye

De daad ai falak, dil-e-hasrat parast kee
Haan, kuchh na kuchh talaafi-e-maafaat chaahiye

Seekhe hain mahrukhon ke liye ham musavviree
Taqreeb kuchh to bahar-e-mulaaqaat chaahiye

Mai se gharaz nishaat hai kis roosiyaah ko
Ik goonah bekhudee mujhe din raat chaahiye

Nashvo numaa hai asla se, Ghalib farogh ko
Khaamoshi hee se nikle hai jo baat chaahiye

53

As near a mosque, a wine-house is necessary
So beneath the brow, an eye is needed

My past is full of unfulfilled desires
O Sky, have mercy on my grief-loving heart

I've cultivated the Muse for the moon-faced ones
But I need a pretext for a meeting with them

Pleasure from wine? Which sinner needs it
I drink day and night to forget myself

As first comes the root, then flowers and fruits
So, Ghalib, first thought, then words from lips

54

Ishq mujhko nahin, vahshat hi sahee
Meri vahshat, teri shohrat hi sahi

Kataa kije na taalluq hamse
Kuchh naheen hai to adaavat hi sahee

Ham bhee dushman to naheen hain apne
Ghair ko tujhse muhabbat hi sahee

Apnee hastee hee se ho jo kuchh ho
Aagahee gar naheen ghaflat hi sahee

Ham bhee tasleem kee khoo daalenge
Beniyaazee tiri aadat hi sahee

Yaar se cherr chalee jaaye Asad
Gar naheen vasl to hasrat hi sahee

54

Yes, my love is not love, it's madness,
Let it bring you fame

Don't break-up with me altogether,
At least, hold on to the thread of hatred

I'm not my own enemy
Even if my rival is in love with you

Let my own self create whatever it wants to,
If I'm not aware, let me enjoy selflessness

Bowing before you is my nature,
Though arrogance be your habit

Let your love encounters continue, Asad,
Even if there be no union, you can still dream

55

Be-etidaaliyon se, subuk sab men ham hue
Jitne ziyaadah ho gaye, utne hi kam hue

Pinhaan thaa daam-e-sakht kareeb aashiyaan ke
Urrne na paaye the ki giriftaar ham hue

Sakhtee kashaan-e-ishq kee, poochhe hai kyaa khabar?
Vo log raftah raftah saraapaa alam hue

Likhte rahe junoon kee hikaayaat-e-khooncha kaan
Harchand usme haath hamaare qalam hue

Chhorree Asad na hamne gadaayee men dillagee
Saa il hue to aashiq-e-ahal-e-karam hue

55

My excesses in love have debased me
The more I've stretched, the shorter I've become

The trap was laid close to my nest
I was caught before I could fly

Why ask, how lovers face their tribulations
By and by, they turn into tokens of grief

I'll keep on extolling their blood-drenched frenzy
Till my hand is amputated and becomes a pen

Even as a beggar, Asad, I hold my sense of fun,
I've fallen in love with my benign patrons

56

Fariyaad kee koyi lai naheen hai
Naalah paaband-e-nai naheen hai

Kyoon bote hain baaghbaan toombe
Gar baagh gadaa-e-mai naheen hai

Harchand harek shai men too hai
Par tujhsee to koyi shai naheen hai

Haan, khaayiyo mat fareb-e-hastee
Harchand kahe ki hai, naheen hai

Shaadee se guzar ki gham na hove
Urdee jo na ho, to dai naheen hai

Kyoon radde qadah kare hai zaahid?
Mai hai, yah magas kee kai naheen hai

Hastee hai, na kuchh adam hai, Ghalib
Aakhir too kyaa hai? Ai naheen hai

56

A prayer may not necessarily have a melody,
A lament may not be in sync with a flute

What good sowing of gourds by the gardener,
If the garden doesn't beg for a bowl of wine?

You are in every thing each moment
Although no thing resembles You.

I won't fall prey to the trap of existence,
It may exist for others, but not for me

You must go beyond joy to wipe all grief,
If there's no spring, how can the autumn be?

Why is the goblet refused by the ascetic?
It holds wine, no vomit of the bees

You neither exist, nor non-exist, Ghalib,
What is there, isn't there, indeed

57

Rone se aur ishq men bebaak ho gaye
Dhoye gaye ham aise ki bas paak ho gaye

Rusvaa-e-dahr go hue, aavaargee se tum
Baare tabeeaton ke to chaalaak ho gaye

Kahtaa hai kaun naalah-e-bulbul ko be-asar
Parde men gul ke laakh jigar chaak ho gaye

Poochhe hai kyaa vajood-o-adam ahal-e-shauq kaa
Aap apnee aag ke khas-o-khaashaak ho gaye

Karne gaye the us se, taghaaful kaa ham gilaa
Kee ek hee nigaah ki bas khaak ho gaye

Is rang se uthaayee kal usne Asad kee laash
Dushman bhee jisko dekh ke ghamnaak ho gaye

57

We wept and opened up further in love
We were so washed, our hearts were cleansed

Your wanderings have made you a laughing stock,
Your life has gained much experience though

Who says, nightingale's cry has been in vain?
In the veil, flower's heart was singed umpteen times

Why ask, what existence lovers' passion has?
They are like fodder to their own fire

I went to her to rant about her indifference
But was turned into dust by her single glance

He lifted Asad's corpse with such fanfare yesterday,
That even his foes were filled with much remorse

58

Kab vo suntaa hai kahaanee meree
Aur phir vo bhi zabaanee meree

Khalish-e-gamzah-e-khoonrez na poochh
Dekh khoonaabah fishaanee meree

Hoon zikhud raftah-e-baidaa-e-khayaal
Bhool jaanaa hai, nishaanee meree

Qadr-e-sang-e-sar-e-rah rakhtaa hoon
Sakht arzaa hai giraanee meree

Gardbaad-e-rah-e-betaabee hoon
Sarsar-e-shauq hai, baanee meree

Kar diyaa zof ne aajiz, Ghalib,
Nang-e-peeree hai, javaanee meree

58

When does He listen to my tale ?
That, too, from my own lips !

Don't ask, how deep her glance has cut
Just look at blood dripping from me

My mind is lost in a wilderness
I'm known for forgetting things

Like a piece of stone by the road –
My worth is of light weight

I'm a whirlwind on the road of anxiety
Passion, like a tempest, rages within me

Too weak, too helpless I am, Ghalib,
My youth is an insult to old age

59

Dil se teri nigaah jigar tak utar gayee
Dono ko ik adaa men razaamand kar gayee

Vo baadah-e-shabaanah kee sarmastiyaan kahaan?
Uthiye bas ab, ki lazzat-e-khvaab-e-sahar gayee

Urrtee phire hai khaak miri, koo-e-yaar men
Baare ab ai havaa, havas-e-baal-o-par gayee

Fardah-o-dee kaa tafrikah yak baar mit gayaa
Kal tum gaye, ki ham pa qayaamat guzar gayee

Maaraa zamaane ne Asadullah Khaan tumhen
Vo valvale kahaan, vo javaanee kidhar gayee?

59

Your glance has pierced my heart and liver –
Both have been won over by a single stroke

Where is intoxication in the night-wine now ?
Arise, there is no delight in dreaming at dawn

My dust keeps loitering in the street of the Beloved,
Wind lacks power to lift it on its wings

The wedge between the past and the future is erased-
Your parting yesterday, has been for me a doomsday

Time has shattered you, Asadullah Khan,
Where's your passion, where has your youth gone?

60

Naved-e-amna hai bedaad-e-dost jaan ke liye
Rahee na tarz-e-sitam koyi aasmaan ke liye

Falak na door rakh us se mujhe, ki main hi nahin
Daraaz dasti-e-qaatil ke imtihaan ke liye

Misaal yah meri koshish kee hai, ki murg-e-aseer
Kare qafas men faraaham khas aashiyaan ke liye

Baqadr-e -shauq nahin, zarf-e-tangnaa-e-ghazal
Kuchh aur chaahiye vus at mire bayaan ke liye

Zabaan pe baar-e-khudaayaa, yah kiskaa naam aayaa
Ki mere nutq ne bose miree zabaan ke liye

Zamaanaa ahad men uske hai mahve-aaraaish
Banenge aur sitaare ab aasmaan ke liye

Varaq tamaan huaa aur madah baaqee hai,
Safeenaa chaahiye is bahr-e- bekaraan ke liye

Adaa-e-khaas se Ghalib huaa hai nuktah saraa
Salaa-e-aam hai yaaraan-e-nuktah daan ke liye

60

Beloved's tyranny is a road I gladly walk
I have no need now for an unkind heaven

O Sky, don't keep me far from her,
I'm not alone to be tested by that slayer

My efforts in life are like a caged bird's
Attempts to gather twigs for his nest

Even the street of ghazal is too narrow,
I require some other mode of expression

Whose name has graced my tongue, O Lord,
That even my voice is kissing my tongue?

Time is about to make decorations in her glory,
More and more stars are appearing in the sky

The page is finished, but my praise for her remains,
A ship is required to cross this boundless ocean

Ghalib, as a poet, bears a style unique,
Friends can take lessons, if they wish

141

61

Main unhen chherroon aur kuchh na kahen
Chal nikalte jo mai piye hote

Kahar ho, yaa balaa ho, jo kuchh ho
Kaash ke tum mire liye hote

Meri kismet men gham gar itnaa thaa
Dil bhee yaa rab kayi diye hote

Aa hee jaataa vo raah par Ghalib
Koyi din aur bhee jiye hote

61

I tease her, she says nothing – what a surprise!
I would've walked away, if I were drunk

A calamity or a disaster - whatever you be
I wish you were for me only

O Lord, if my fate has to bear so much grief,
You should've also gifted me many, many hearts

He would've finally come to terms, Ghalib,
If only I had lived some days more

62

Hazaaron khvaahishen aisi, ki har khvaahish pe dam nikle
Bahut nikle mire armaan, lekin phir bhi kam nikle

Nikalnaa Khuld se Aadam kaa sunte aaye the lekin
Bahot be-aabroo hokar tire kooche se ham nikle

Magar likhvaaye koyi usko khat to hamse likhvaaye
Huyi subah, aur ghar se kaan par rakh kar qalam nikle

Huyi jinse tavakko, khastagee kee daad paane kee
Vo hamse bhi ziyaadah khastah-e-tegh-e-sitam nikle

Khudaa ke vaaste pardaa na Kaabe kaa uthaa zaalim
Kaheen aisaa na ho yaan bhee vahee kaafir sanam nikle

Kahaan maikhaane kaa darvaazah, Ghalib, aur kahaan vaaiz
Par itnaa jaante hain, kal vo jaataa thaa ki ham nikle

62

A thousand desires I had, each enough to take my breath
Many longings were fulfilled, yet these were not enough

Adam was driven from Paradise - I've long heard that tale
A disgrace far more worse has been my exit from your lane

I'll help if you want a letter to be written to her
For, since morn, I've been roaming with a pen on my ear

When I expect that someone will show sympathy for my plight
He turns out to be more wounded by the blade of misfortune

O tyrant, for God's sake, don't lift the curtain of Kaaba
Or else the same unfaithful icon may appear there, too

Where's the door of tavern, Ghalib? What has the priest to do with it?
This much I know that yesterday, as I came out he entered it !

Part III

1

Naqsh fariyaadee hai kiskee shokhiye tahreer kaa
Kaaghazee hai pairahan, har paikar-e-tasveer kaa

The picture is a plaintiff of which Beauty's mischievousness?
Each image is to be found here robed in a papery dress

2

Kaave-kaave sakhtjaaneehaa-e-tanhaayee na pooch
Subah karnaa sham kaa, laanaa hai joo-e-sheer kaa

Scratch me not repeatedly for my life's loneliness and woe,
Dawn to dusk I've been trying for a channel of milk to flow !

3

Ba faiz-e-bedilee, naumeedi-e-jaaved aasaan hai
Kashaaish ko hamaaraa uqdah-e-mushkil pasand aayaa

My thanks to pessimism, eternal hopelessness hangs on me light
Much pleased I am that I've no wish to open the twisted knots
of life

4

Ishq se tabeeyat ne zeest kaa mazaa paayaa
Dard kee davaa payee, dard-e-bedavaa paayaa

Where to seek the fun of life? Love has revealed for sure
I have found the cure for pain, in pain without a cure

5

Siyaahee jaise gir jaaye dam-e-tahreer kaaghaz par
Miree kismat men yoon tasveer hai shab haa-e-hizraan kee

Drops of ink having fallen on the paper while writing -
In my fate, nights of parting are such picture presenting !

6

Kis se mahroomi-e-kismat kee shikaayat keeje
Hamne chaahaa thaa ki mar jaayen, so vo bhee na huaa

Whom should I complain, about my Fate betraying me
I had wished for Death, even that was denied to me

7

Muhabbat thee chaman se, lekin ab yah bedimaaghee hai
Ki mauj-e-boo-e-gul se naak men aataa hai dam meraa

I once loved the garden, but now I'm so out of mind,
That the flowers' fragrance, too nauseating I do find.

8

Ab main hoon aur maatame yak shahar-e-aarzoo
Torraa jo toone aainah timsaaldaar thaa

I'm left to mourn for a city of ravaged desires-
The mirror and its images, you have shattered to pieces

9

Saraapaa rehan-e-ishq-o-naaguzeer-e-ulfat-e-hastee
Ibaadat barq kee kartaa hoon aur afsos haasil kaa

I've pledged myself to love, and also hold dear my life –
Like someone who worships lightning and regrets its outcome, too.

10

Junnaar baandh, subh-e-saddaanaa torr daal
Rahrau chale hai raah ko, hamvaar dekh kar

Break the rosary beads and put on the sacred thread;
The even road is easy for a traveller to tread.

11

Bas ki dushvaar hai, har kaam kaa aasaan honaa
Aadmee ko bhee mayassar naheen insaan honaa

Even a task that looks easy, can prove to be a difficult thing
Indeed, it's hard for any man to be a simple human being !

12

Faayadah kyaa? Soch, aakhir too bhee daanaa hai Asad
Dostee naadaan kee hai, jee kaa ziyaan ho jaayegaa

What gain is there? Think; you are too naive, Asad,
The friendship of the fool will only ruin your heart.

13

Dil meraa soz-e-nihaan se bemahaabaa jal gayaa
Aatash-e-khaamosh kee maanind goyaa jal gayaa

The fire raging within me has burnt my heart entire;
It's as if it has been through fireworks without a sound.

14

Dil men zauq-e-vasl-o-yaad-e-yaar tak baaqee naheen
Aag is ghar men lagee aisee, ki jo thaa jal gayaa

I have no desire to meet her, her memory has left my heart
All things have turned into ash, this house has been on fire !

15

Main hoon aur afsurdagee kee aarzoo, Ghalib ki dil
Dekh kar tarz-e-tapaak-e-ahal-e-duniyaa jal gayaa

I am left alone with my yearning for despondency,
Ghalib, this world's ire has burnt my heart completely.

16

Ishrat-e-qatrah hai, dariyaa men fanaa ho jaanaa
Dard kaa had se guzarnaa hai davaa ho jaanaa

A drop by merging into the sea, attains its bliss;
Pain becomes a panacea, when it crosses all limits.

17

Khamoshee men nihaan khoongashtah laakhon aarzooen hain
Charaagh-e-murdaa hoon main bezabaan gor-e-ghareebaan kaa

To the slaying of a million desires, I've been a silent witness:
I am a lamp extinguished, in the graveyard of the mute and
helpless.

18

Go na samjhoon uskee baaten, go na paaoon uskaa bhed
Par yah kyaa kam hai ki mujhse vo pari-paikar khulaa

Although I can't understand her words, nor the secrets of her
mind,
Is it less important that, that angelic face has turned towards me?

19

Uskee ummat men hoon main, mere rahen kyoon kaam band
Vaaste jis shah ke Ghalib gumbad-e-bedar khulaa

When I am of his faith, Ghalib, why won't my plans materialise -
That Prophet, who was welcomed by the doorless dome of
Paradise

20

Raat din gardish men hain saat aasmaan
Ho rahegaa kuchh na kuchh, ghabraayen kyaa?

Day and night, the seven skies swirl and swirl
When something is bound to happen, why to fear?

21

Hai zavaal-aamaadah azzaa aafareenish ke tamaam
Mehr-e-gadoo hai charaagh-e-rahguzaar-e-baad,yaan

All elements of nature are destined to decay,
The sun is here like a lamp in whirlwind's way

154

22

Dekhiye, paate hain ushshaaq, buton se kyaa faiz
Ik Birahmin ne kahaa hai ki yah saal achchhaa hai

Let us see, what boon from idols, lovers will get this year,
'All the best '- is all that I from a Brahmin hear.

23

Lo ham mareez-e-ishq ke teemaardaar hain
Achchhaa agar na ho, to Maseehaa kaa kyaa ilaaj?

Look, we'll treat him, who falls sick with passion
But if he still can't get well, what cure by Jesus then?

24

Shamma bujhtee hai to usme se dhuaan uthtaa hai
Sholah-e-ishq siyahposh huaa mere baad

When the candle is extinguished, it releases smoke
So after me, the flame of love will don a black cloak

25

Aaye hai bekasi-e-ishq pe ronaa Ghalib
Kiske ghar jaayegaa, sailaab-e-balaa mere baad

I weep at the helplessness of love, Ghalib,
Whose house this flood of woes go to, after me?

26

Yaarab, vo na samjhe hain, na samjhenge miri baat
De aur dil unko, jo na de mujhko zabaan aur

O Lord, she hasn't understood, nor will understand what I say,
Bless her with another heart, or gift me another tongue

27

Gar tujhko hai yakeen-e-ijaabat, duaa na maang
Yaanee bighair-e-yak dil-e-bemudduaa na maang

Don't ask for a boon, if sure you are that the Lord will grant;
If you've to ask, ask only for a heart without desire.

28

Loon vaam bakht-e-khuft se, yak khvaab-e-khush vale
Ghalib, yah khauf hai ki kahaan se adaa karoon

I will borrow a sweet dream from my sleeping Fate;
But, Ghalib, my fear is : how I'll return this debt?

29

Partav-e-khur se hai shabnam ko fanaa kee taaleem
Main bhee hoon ik inayat kee nazar hone tak

The dew takes its lesson of death from sun's radiance;
I too exist till I receive Thy gracious glance.

30

Nagmah haa-e-gham ko bhee, ai dil ghaneemat jaaniye
Besadaa ho jaayegaa, yah saaz-e-hastee ek din

Know even the songs of heart in grief, to be a gift of fortune
For, this lyre of existence would one day be without its tune

31

Ho gayee hai ghair kee sheereen bayaanee kaargar
Ishq kaa usko gumaan ham bezabaano par naheen

The sweet words of my rival have cast their spell –
She has no inkling of my love, for I'm tongue-tied.

32

Is saadagee pe kaun na mar jaaye, ai Khudaa
Larrte hain aur haath men talvaar bhee naheen

O God, who won't like to be slain by her simplicity?
She fights without wielding a sword in her hand

33

Vo aaye ghar men hamaare, Khudaa kee qudrat hai
Kabhee ham unko, kabhee apne ghar ko dekhte hai

She has stepped into my home - that is God's grace;
Sometimes at her, sometimes my home, I turn my gaze !

34

Qatrah dariyaa men jo mil jaaye, to dariyaa ho jaaye,
Kaam achchhaa hai vo jiskaa ki ma-aal achchhaa hai

A drop that mingles with the ocean, becomes an ocean;
A task is worthy, indeed, whose outcome is good.

35

Lakhnau aane kaa vaais naheen khultaa, yaanee
Havas-e-sair-o-tamaashaa, so vo kam hai hamko

For my coming to Lucknow, no reason do I see,
The wish for tour and spectacle is hardly left in me.

36

Nuktacheen hai, gham-e-dil unko sunaaye na bane
Kyaa bane baat jahaan baat banaaye na bane

My Love is always questioning, how can my heart's woe
I tell her?
Indeed, it is too difficult to spin a story before her.

37

Tum jaano, tumko gair se jo rasm-o-raah ho
Mujhko bhee poochhte raho to kyaa gunaah ho?

You may go to meet my rival, I shall leave that to you;
But tell me, will it be wrong if you care for me, too?

38

Ghalib kuchh apnee sai se lahnaa naheen mujhe
Khirman jale agar na malakh khaaye kisht ko

Ghalib, though much I persevere, my toil goes all in vain
If locusts don't come to eat, lightning burns all my grain.

39

Us chashm-e-fusoongar kaa agar paaye ishaaraa
Tootee kee tarah aainah guftaar men aave

If the magic of the Beloved's eye is working,
Like a parrot, the mirror will start twittering.

40

Na lut taa din ko to kab raat ko yoon bekhabar sotaa
Rahaa khatkaa na choree kaa, duaa detaa hoon rahjan ko

If I weren't robbed in broad daylight, I wouldn't have slept so
well at night;
I have no fear of theft any more, I wish that the brigand is all
right.

41

Sukhan kyaa kah naheen sakte ki joyaa hon javaahir ke
Jigar kyaa ham naheen rakhte ki khoden jaa ke maadan ko

When we can write verses, why should we seek the pearls?
Is there no heart in us, that we should dig the mines?

42

Hastee ke mat fareb men aa jaayiyo Asad
Aalam tamaam halkah-e-daam-e-khayaal hai

Don't get deceived by your existence, Asad,
The world around you is a maze of imagination.

43

Khultaa kisi ke dil pe kyoon mire dil kaa muaamlah
Sheron ke intikhaab ne rusvaa kiyaa mujhe

How could have anyone known, what was in my mind?
The verses that I chose, have left me only maligned

44

Yoon hee dukh kisee ko denaa naheen khoob, varnah kahtaa
Ki mire adoo ko, Yaarab, mile meri zindagaanee

It's not good to simply give pain to someone, otherwise
I would have prayed: O God, give my rival, my life !

45

Na sitaaish kee tamannaa, na sile kee parvaah
Gar naheen hain mire ashaar men maanee, na sahee

I don't crave for praise, nor that reward should come to me,
If the meaning of my verse is not clear, then let it be

46

Bojh vo sir pe giraa hai ki uthaaye na uthe
Kaam vo aan parraa hai ki banaaye na bane

The burden that has fallen on my head, I can't bear it;
The task that has come to my hand, I can't accomplish

47

Aagosh-e-gul kushudah baraa-e-biddaay hai
Ai andaleeb chal, ki chale din bahaar ke

The rose opens up her arms for the parting embrace;
O nightingale, move on now, the spring has run its race

48

Kahoon kyaa dil kee kyaa haalat hai, hijr-e-yaar men, Ghalib,
Ki betaabee se, har ik taar-e-bistaar khaar-e-bistar hai

Ghalib, I can't tell, how in separation from the Beloved my
heart is suffering;
Restlessness has made each thread of the bedding, a thorn in
the bedding.

49

Ishq par zor nahin hai yah vo aatish, Ghalib,
Ki lagaaye na lage aur bujhaaye na bane

Love's a fire that can't be controlled, Ghalib,
It's hard to lit, and once lit, can't be extinguished.

50

Dillagee kee aarzoo bechain rakhtee hai hame,
Varnah yon be-raunaqee sood-e-charaagh-e-kushtah hai

Our desire for union, keeps our soul tormented ;
If we hadn't so desired, it would have been better.

51

Pach aa parree hai vaadah-e-dildaar kee mujhe
Vo aaye yaa na aaye, pa yon intizaar hai

I stand by the Beloved's promise of coming;
He may come, or may not come – I am waiting.

52

Ghalib buraa na maan jo vaaiz buraa kahe
Aisaa bhee koyi hai ki sab achchhaa kahen jise

Ghalib, don't be peeved if the critic assails you,
Is there anyone in the world, who gets praised by all?

53

Ho ke aashiq vo pareerukh aur naazuk ban gayaa
Rang khultaa jaaye hai, jitnaa ki urrtaa jaaye hai

Love struck, that angelic face has become more delicate;
Fairer it gets, the more its colour does fade

54

Go main rahaa raheen-e-sitamahaa-e-rozgaar
Lekin tire khayaal se ghaafil naheen rahaa

Although I have passed my life, pledged to Time's cruelty,
Yet Your thought, O Beloved, has never forsaken me

55

Bekhudee besabab naheen, Ghalib
Kuchh to hai jiskee pardahdaaree hai

This forgetfulness is not without a reason, Ghalib,
There is, indeed, some secret beneath the veil.

56

Ganjeenah-e-maanee kaa tilism usko samajhiye
Jo lafz ki Ghalib mire ash-aar men aave

Take it as a talisman to meaning's treasury,
The word that, Ghalib, enters into my poetry

57

Hoon mai bhee tamaashaayee –e-nairang-e-tamannaa
Matlab naheen kuchh is se ke matlab hee bar aave

I too am a spectator to Desire's magical display
Whether it serves any purpose at all, I can't say

58

Naheen kuchh subhah-o-zunnaar ke fande men geeraai,
Vafaadaaree men Shaikh-o-Birahman kee aazmaaish hai

The noose of the rosary and the sacred thread, is too weak,
The true test of the Sheikh and the Brahmin, is in their faith.

59

Maikhaanaa-e-jigar men yahaan khaaq bhee nahin,
Khamiyaazaa khenche hai but-e-bedaadafan hanoz

In my liver's tavern now there is left nothing;
Yet with thirst is that tormenting idol yawning !

60

Ug rahaa hai dar-o-deevaar pe sabzah, Ghalib,
Ham bayaabaan men hain aur ghar men bahaar aayee hai

Ghalib, at the doorway and on walls the grass is growing
I'm drought-affected, while my house enjoys the spring!

61

Zindagee jab apnee is shakl se guzree Ghalib
Ham bhee kyaa yaad karenge ki Khudaa rakhte the

Ghalib when my life has been through such a rot,
May I well remember, I too had a God?

62

Ghalib, tiraa ahvaal sunaa denge ham unko
Vo sun ke bulaa len, yah izaarah nahin karte

Ghalib, your plight I'll narrate to her ;
Whether she'll call you, I can't assure

63

Jabki tum bin naheen koyi maujood
Phir yah hangaamah, ai Khudaa, kyaa hai?

When nothing in the world exists without You,
Tell me, O God, why's all this hullabaloo?

64

Na teer kamaan men hai, na saiyyaad kamee men
Goshe men kafas ke mujhe aaraam bahut hai

No arrow is on the bow, no fowler lies in wait;
I'm quite comfortable, within the confines of my cage.

65

Khoon hoke jigar aankh se tapkaa naheen, ai marg
Rahne de mujhe yaan ki abhee kaam bahot hai

The blood of my heart has yet to drip from my eyes,
O Death, spare me, for I have still much work to do

66

Kahoon jo haal to kahte ho mudduaa kahiye
Tumhee kaho ki jo tum yoon kaho, to kyaa kahiye?

Whenever I my plight narrate,
You say, 'come to the point straight';
When to me you talk that way,
Tell me then, what can I say?

67

Safeenah jabki kinaare pa aa lagaa, Ghalib,
Khudaa se kyaa sitam-e-jor-e-naakhudaa kahiye

Ghalib, when on the shore, my ship has arrived already,
Why to rant before God, the pilot's idiosyncracy?

68

Khat likhenge garche matlab kuchh na ho,
Ham to aashiq hain tumhaare naam ke

I shall write letters to you without a cause,
For, I am enamoured just by your name.

69

Ishq ne Ghalib nikammaa kar diyaa
Varnah ham bhee aadmee the kaam ke

Love has made me good-for-nothing, Ghalib,
Otherwise I too was once, a man of substance

170

70

Sabze ko jab kaheen jagah na milee
Ban gayaa roo-e-aab par kaayee

When the green grass couldn't find anymore space,
It turned itself into moss on water's surface

71

Hamko maaloom hai zannat kee haqeeqat, lekin
Dil ke khush rakhne ko Ghalib yeh khayaal achchhaa hai

Yes, I know what is Heaven's reality;
Yet its notion, Ghalib, keeps my heart happy.

72

Dil diyaa jaan ke kyoon usko vafaadaar Asad
Galtee kee ki jo Kaafir ko Musalmaan samjhaa

Why I thought she would be faithful? Why I offered her my heart?
To view that Kafir as a Muslim, was a blunder on my part.

73

Boo-e-gul, naalah-e-dil, dood-e-charaagh-e-mehfil
Jo tiri bazm se niklaa, so pareeshaan niklaa

The flower's fragrance, heart's sigh and lamp's smoke –
Whatever went out of your assembly, went out broke

74

Shahaadat thee miri kismet men, jo dee thee yah khoo mujhko
Jahaan talvaar ko dekhaa, jhukaa detaa thaa gardan ko

I was born to be a martyr, that's the will of God,
Whenever a sword flashed, my neck has bowed.

75

Jo aaoon saamne unke, to marhabaa na kahen
Jo jaaoon vaan se kaheen ko, to khairbaad naheen

When I come before her, she has no 'welcome' to offer;
Nor a 'good-bye' or 'take care', when I take leave of her.

76

Hamaare zahan men, is fikr kaa hai naam visaal
Ki gar na ho to kahaan jaayen, ho to kyunkar ho?

In my mind, union with the Beloved is a perturbing thought;
If it is not there, what then? If it comes about, then what?

77

Dekhnaa taqreer kee lazzat, ki jo usne kahaa
Maine yah jaanaa ki goyaa yah bhee mere dil men hai

How sweet my Friend's speech ! Whatever I hear him say,
Exactly the same feeling, my heart seems to portray.

78

Vahee ik baat hai, jo yaan nafas, vaan nakhat-e-gul hai
Chaman kaa jalvah vaais hai mire rangeen navaayee kaa

The words I breathe and the rose's scent, are one and the same;
My song blooms when the garden blooms.

79

Tum unke vaade kaa zikr unse kyoon karo Ghalib,
Yah kyaa ki tum kaho, aur vo kahen ki yaad naheen ?

Why should you remind her, Ghalib, of the promise made
by her?
What if you say it, and she says, she doesn't remember?

80

Sau baar band-e-ishq se aazaad ham huey,
Par kyaa Karen, ki dil hee adoo hai faraagh kaa

A hundred times from love-shackles, I have broken free;
But what to do? My own heart is freedom's enemy.

81

Kaabe men jaa rahaa, to na do taanah, kyaa kaheen
Bhoolaa hoon haqq-e-sohbat-e-kunisht ko?

Don't taunt Me, if it is the Kaaba, I have come to rest;
No question that those who seek Me in the temple, I'll forget.

82

Vaarastagee bahaanah-e-begaangee naheen
Apne se kar, na ghair se, vahshat hee kyoon na ho

By pretending aloofness, it doesn't mean you are free;
Shun yourself, not others, even if madness it be.

83

Na pooch vus-at-e-maikhaanah-e-junoon Ghalib,
Jahaan yah kaasah-e-gadoo, hai ek khaaq andaaz

Ask not, whether the tavern of my madness has its limit,
Ghalib, the bowl of the sky is just a dustbin before it.

84

Hain aur bhee dunyaa men sukhanvar bahut achchhe
Par kahte hain ki Ghalib kaa hai andaaz-e-bayaan aur

Many poets in the world have cast a good impression,
But it is said, Ghalib is unique in his expression.

85

Aate hain ghaib se, yeh mazaamee khayaal men
Ghalib, sareer-e-khaamah navaa-e-sarosh hai

These verses that I write, descend from some Unseen Power;
The sound that my quill releases, is an angel's whisper.

86

Zahar-e-gham kar chukaa thaa meraa kaam
Tumko kisne kahaa ki ho bad naam

The poison of grief had already finished me,
Who told you to share the blame?

87

Aazaad rau hoon aur miraa maslak hai sulh-e-kul
Hargiz kabhee kisee se adaavat naheen mujhe
Saadiq hoon apne qaul men, Ghalib, Khudaagavaah
Kahtaa hoon sach ki jhoot kee aadat naheen mujhe

A free breeze I am, in friendship with all,
I have no ill-will towards anyone;
By God, I'm true to my word, Ghalib,
Truthfully I say: I don't speak untruth at all.

88

Mushkil hai jibas kalaam meraa ai dil
Sun sun ke use sukhanvaraan-e-kaamil
Aasaan karne kee karte hain farmaayish
Goyam mushkil, vagar na goyam mushkil

O Dear, I do agree that my ghazals are hard to comprehend,
Even learned poets wish that I should adopt the easy way;
But what to do? I only write that which is difficult to say.

89

Dahar juz jalvah-e-yaktaai-e-maashooq naheen
Ham kahaan hote, agar husn na hotaa khudbeen.
Harzah hai naghmah-e-zeer-o-bam-e-hasti-o-adam
Laghva hai aainah-e-firq-e-junoon-o-tamkeen.
Laaf-e-daanish ghalat-o-nafa-e-ibaadat maaloom
Durd-e-yak saaghar-e-ghaflat hai che duniyaa-o-che deen.

In the world the Beloved has manifested Himself uniquely,
If His Beauty wasn't Self-seeking, we wouldn't be existing.
At each place and time is the cacophony of 'is' and 'is not';
Madness and self-possession have, in the mirror, no meaning
Knowledge is not all, nor is the fruit of worship known;
Last drops are World and Faith in the cup of unknowing.

90

Tum jiyo hazaaron saal
Saal ke din hon pachaas hazaar

May you live long for thousands of years
May each year be of days fifty-thousand

Other work in translation by Sunil Uniyal ~

'The Target is Behind the Sky- Fifty Poems of Kabir'
(Books for All, Low Price Publications, Delhi, 2012)

Some Opinions:

"Steeped in the culture and philosophy of the sub-continent, these translations by Sunil Uniyal, lose none of the profundity, mysticism and philosophy of their author in translation – suggesting a thorough and sympathetic understanding of the material, a 'feel' for its nuances and inferences, by the translator....For students of Kabir, or those new to the rich and diverse poetry of the Indian poets, this is a MUST read." - **Michael Sullivan**, the British poet, City of Plymouth's first Poet Laureate and author of *In a Mirror Darkly, A Cup O' Nails,* etc.

"Sunil Uniyal brings to life the poems or 'utterances' of the Hindi mystic Kabir. The translations beautifully evoke Kabir's imaginative yet down-to-earth writings and give welcome glimmers of the awakenings, the medieval poet hoped to encourage." – **Donna Baier Stein**, Writer and Editor, Tiferet Journal, Sept. 11, 2012.